D1583936

Mosquito

by date shown

Animal
Series editor: Jonathan Burt

Already published

Ant Charlotte Sleigh · *Ape* John Sorenson · *Bear* Robert E. Bieder
Bee Claire Preston · *Camel* Robert Irwin · *Cat* Katharine M. Rogers
Chicken Annie Potts · *Cockroach* Marion Copeland · *Cow* Hannah Velten
Crow Boria Sax · *Dog* Susan McHugh · *Donkey* Jill Bough
Duck Victoria de Rijke · *Eel* Richard Schweid · *Elephant* Daniel Wylie
Falcon Helen Macdonald · *Fly* Steven Connor · *Fox* Martin Wallen
Frog Charlotte Sleigh · *Giraffe* Mark Williams · *Hare* Simon Carnell
Horse Elaine Walker · *Hyena* Mikita Brottman · *Kangaroo* John Simons
Lion Deirdre Jackson · *Lobster* Richard J. King · *Moose* Kevin Jackson
Mosquito Richard Jones · *Otter* Daniel Allen · *Owl* Desmond Morris
Oyster Rebecca Stott · *Parrot* Paul Carter · *Peacock* Christine E. Jackson
Penguin Stephen Martin · *Pig* Brett Mizelle · *Pigeon* Barbara Allen
Rat Jonathan Burt · *Rhinoceros* Kelly Enright · *Salmon* Peter Coates
Shark Dean Crawford · *Snail* Peter Williams · *Snake* Drake Stutesman
Sparrow Kim Todd · *Spider* Katja and Sergiusz Michalski · *Swan* Peter Young
Tiger Susie Green · *Tortoise* Peter Young · *Trout* James Owen
Vulture Thom Van Dooren · *Whale* Joe Roman · *Wolf* Garry Marvin

Mosquito

Richard Jones

REAKTION BOOKS

Published by
REAKTION BOOKS LTD
33 Great Sutton Street
London EC1V 0DX, UK
www.reaktionbooks.co.uk

First published 2012
Copyright © Richard Jones 2012

All rights reserved

No part of this publication may be reproduced, stored in a retrieval
system or transmitted, in any form or by any means, electronic,
mechanical, photocopying, recording or otherwise without the prior
permission of the publishers.

Printed and bound in China by C&C Offset Printing Co., Ltd

British Library Cataloguing in Publication Data
Jones, Richard, 1958 July 14-
    Mosquito. – (Animal)
    1. Mosquitoes. 2. Mosquitoes as carriers of disease.
    3. Malaria – Epidemiology.
    I. Title II. Series
    595.7'72-DC23

ISBN 978 1 86189 923 1

Contents

Introduction

A high-pitched whine – whisper-quiet, but nerve-tingling – drills through the still night air, rousing the fitful sleeper. It's no use flapping with arms or a rolled-up magazine: this is one insect that will not go away. The mosquito is on a mission. It wants blood, and will not give up without a fight.

Bloodsucking insects have tormented humans for hundreds of thousands of years, and before that they pestered *Australo-pithecus*, Neanderthals and all the other protohumans. This long-standing intimate battle for our blood has had several consequences. The bloodsuckers have had to outwit swatting and grooming by surreptitious attack. Their small size and quiet stealth has made them seem vindictive and malevolent. They have had to cope with the defensive mechanism of human blood clotting when they suck. And it is what they leave behind when they bite – the allergic reaction to their injection and the disease organisms injected – that has caused so much human suffering. It means that, over the centuries, whereas most small insects were lumped together and called simply 'bug', 'fly', 'worm' or 'beetle', bloodsuckers were much more precisely identified and given names. Fleas, lice, gads, stouts, ticks, clegs and keds are just some of the many names in English alone. The slim flies that were particularly aggressive have long been called gnats or midges, but towards the end of the sixteenth century the English started to adopt the name 'mosquito' from their seafaring competitors the Spanish and the Portuguese. This is a name now known throughout the world, and it is loaded with meaning.

In much of the 'Western', developed world, or at least in its major metropolitan centres, mosquitoes are still derided as a trivial nuisance: they bite. But Western urbanites have short memories. Even a generation or two ago, mosquitoes would have been associated with a broader insanitary mess of creatures that invaded homes, attacked food and belongings and even threatened lives with filth and disease. In such homes today, vacuum cleaners have done away with the human flea and the carpet beetle; man-made fibres and dry-cleaning have controlled the clothes moth; refrigerators have rid us of larder beetles; Tupperware and cling film (along with double glazing and improved sanitation) have reduced the horribly diverse disease threat from houseflies. Today, our urban homes are mostly insect-free.

So, an insect that can smell us through a bedroom window barely ajar, fly in on silken wings that don't rustle the curtains and target us with secret sneak attack, is rather unnerving. But we should thank our lucky stars and our sanitized surroundings that all we have to worry about is a vague pinprick and the loss of a tiny dribble of blood. All that remains is a red spot for a day or two.

In many parts of the world, though, mosquitoes are still arguably the most dangerous animals on the planet. Mosquitoes spread the tiny protozoan parasites that cause malaria, and several other deadly and debilitating diseases. Malaria infects over 200 million people worldwide and is estimated to kill nearly 1 million people each year. Most of these are young children living in sub-Saharan Africa. To borrow a well-known but nevertheless awful analogy from Tanzanian malaria researcher Wen

Scanning electron micrograph of the head of *Anopheles gambiae*, arguably the most dangerous animal in the world.

Kilama, that's like seven Boeing 747s loaded with children crashing into mountains every day of the year.

The malarial belt around the world's tropics has long been a dangerous place to visit. And although it is perhaps stretching a euphemism, for most of that lush zone between Cancer and Capricorn, white people are still 'visitors', at least in terms of human evolutionary history. For nearly 500 years, since the dawn of the Age of Exploration, European travellers to the tropics were tormented by mosquitoes and ravaged by malarial fevers. This irked the colonial powers, who saw malaria as a barrier to their 'civilizing' influences. When the nature of mosquitoes as disease vectors was elucidated, a way was suddenly opened to clear these fertile lands for exploitation and commerce. Eradicating the mosquitoes was simply a case of destroying their swampy breeding grounds.

We've known about the intricate relationship between mosquitoes and malaria for over 100 years. Mosquito-control programmes have been put in place, and anti-malarial drugs have been available for over two centuries. But mosquitoes do not respect international boundaries, and are quick to take advantage of both petty political differences and all-out war. A change in government, a change in the annual rainfall, even a change in the stock markets a hemisphere away, can easily set such ambitious schemes back decades.

It transpires that national governments and international aid agencies do not have bottomless pockets, and eradicating malaria has turned out to be very expensive. Mass spraying with insecticides has turned out to be environmentally damaging, and the backlash against chemicals like DDT has removed what was seen at the time as the most promising weapon in the war against mosquitoes. Drug resistance in the malaria parasites and insecticide resistance in the mosquitoes is just the latest turn of a battle that has shaped the history of humans on this planet. Talk now moves away from removing the malarial threat entirely, and attention focuses increasingly on containment, mitigation and management. These are coping strategies on the back foot. Mosquitoes are still winning the war.

1 Will it Bite?

Bloodsucking insects have been biting humans for countless thousands of years, but as our understanding of their different types has developed, one group has come to acquire a sinister notoriety far beyond their diminutive size. Today, the narrow-winged, thin-bodied, long-legged flies that pester us in the night or in marshy fields are almost universally called 'mosquito'. This name is recognizable around the world in a wide number of languages: *mosquito* in English, Spanish and Portuguese, *mosquit* in Catalan, *moustique* in French, *Moskito* in German, *Moschgieder* in Deitsch (Pennsylvania German), *mosgito* in Welsh, *muiscít* in Gaelic, *moskítóflugur* in Icelandic and *mushkonja* in Shqip (Albanian). But 'mosquito' is a relatively modern appellation, appearing (in English at least) only at the very end of the sixteenth century. The bite victim, left rubbing a swollen welt, might wonder why it matters what we call the bug that bit, and why it should be at all important to distinguish it from other biters. The scientist provides the answer. It is not so much the prick given, or the blood taken, but the disease left behind after the bite that has defined mosquitoes and made them among the most vilified creatures on the planet. In this instance, it becomes supremely important what we call things, and how we distinguish them from one another.

Things were not always so. When the first 'cave men' fell victim to bloodsucking flies, they would no doubt have given their tormentors names – names to discuss them civilly, or to curse them by. These names are now hidden in the clouds of prehistory, and a study of biting insect names can only really begin with the first written texts, or at least those texts that are preserved.

The ancients of classical Greece and Rome made very unclear distinctions between the various sorts of small, biting flies. Aelian, writing in the second century, claimed that African biting flies were larger and more aggressive than those in the Mediterranean. The upside of this was that, although they attacked humans with greater voracity, they also helped to keep lions away. Like most classical authors, he does not give quite enough information to identify exactly which flies he is talking about. For several hundred years, observers refer to various small, nondescript biting flies, and names like *empis*, *culex* and *conops* are regularly bandied about.[1] Unhelpfully, these names are also applied to other insects, which, from the context, are obviously not biting flies at all. Sometimes, it is virtually impossible to equate these archaic terms with modern names. Aristotle has been criticized for ignoring gnats, but this is rather unfair given that so many small insects are still, today, lumped together by non-specialists as just 'bugs'. He knew well enough that some insects have their stings in front (for feeding) or behind (as a weapon) and that no two-winged insect (fly) had its sting behind, because these insects are too weak to sting with their abdomens. Pliny repeated that gnats had their sting at the oral orifice. Biting and stinging are still confused today.

Language scholars still struggle to interpret exactly what creatures appear in classical literature. A salutary example is shown by trying to understand the biblical plagues, rained down by a wrathful Old Testament God. The third plague is variously translated as one of 'nits' or 'gnats'. These two very similar-sounding words in English may have similar roots, but they relate to entirely different creatures. The fourth plague is often referred to as a plague of flies, but 'beetles', and 'wild beasts' are also used in some understandings. The English entomologist John Obadiah Westwood was one of the first (1838) to suggest that it was actually a plague of 'musquitoes'.[2] His supposition was based on a knowledge of insect ecology, rather than linguistic expertise, but the debate is still ongoing. The Bible is one of the most intensively studied texts in the world and yet modern experts in history and linguistics still cannot agree exactly what was meant. To get an understanding of the names we now use for biting insects, we really have to start in the present (or at most in the past two or three hundred years), and work backwards, extrapolating as best we can until the linguistic threads are frayed and lost.

WHAT'S IN A NAME?

Naming insects has often been a vague process. We have general terms for those that are startling (dragonfly), pretty (butterfly) or inspirational (sacred scarab), or that are nuisance pests that attack homes (termite), crops (locust), timber (woodworm), food (housefly) or other human belongings (bookworm). Most insects are secretive, avoiding human contact, and have gone without precise names for millennia, until modern scientists began to catalogue them as part of their esoteric studies into biodiversity.

Bloodsucking insects, though, do often have good, solid common names; this is because they came to the notice of the humans they bit very early on in history. Most of these names show folk origins from simple word roots. Thus, in English alone we have a veritable wealth of names to choose from: flea (familiar jumping insects); louse (also sometimes nit); bedbug (bites us in our beds); mite (a widely used alternative for flea, louse and others); tick (bloodsucking arachnid); cleg, stout, gadfly and breeze (all bloodsucking flies of stock animals and their herders); horsefly (also bites their riders); stablefly (also bites the grooms); sandfly (lives in sandy places); deerfly (also bites their stalkers); sheep ked (on sheep, and the occasional shepherd); blackfly (some are also grey); and, in North America especially, the jauntily named no-see-um (virtually any tiny, biting fly).

Across the world, these same, or similar, bloodsuckers have national, local and dialect names aplenty. In various parts of England, for example, residents are bothered by buers or buvers (the northeast), mingins (Norfolk) and nudges (Cheshire).[3] Traditionally, the more delicate, flimsy, diaphanous bloodsuckers have been called, in English, midge or gnat. These two lovely, short, monosyllabic words, which can be sneered or spat out, tell us much about the opinions our ancestors had for these unlovely insects.

'Midge', descended through the Old English *mycg*, Old Saxon *muggia*, Old High German *mucca* and Norse *my*, seems to be a corruption from the Latin *musca* – 'fly'. J.R.R. Tolkien immediately evoked the buggy itchiness of the swamplands by having his *Lord of the Rings* (1954–5) hobbit heroes trudge through the Midgewater Marshes on the first leg of their epic journey through Middle-earth. 'There are more midges than water!' protests an irate Peregrin Took. Thomas Hardy's unnamed woman-of-the-road, in his poem 'A Trampwoman's Tragedy' (1903), was bitten 'by every Marshwood midge'. In Robert Louis Stevenson's *Kidnapped* (1886), the narrator David Balfour is 'troubled by a cloud of stinging midges'.

'Gnat' comes from the Old English *gnaett*, Low German *gnatte* and Middle Low German *gnitte*, which some etymologists have also linked to the nit. Gnat is possibly a shortening of one of the words the ancient Greeks used for various biting flies: *conops* (κωνωψ), literally 'cone-faced', alluding to the insects' pointed heads.[4] Unfortunately, the modern fly genus *Conops* has nothing to do with pointy-faced bloodsuckers, but refers instead to a group of pretty, wasp-like bee parasites. But there is an ancient echo in the language, since a couch or bed protected by a mosquito net was, in Roman times, *conopium*, from which we get canopy and canapé (covered bread).[5]

Gnat, even more than midge, seems to have been used historically in a much more diffuse way than some of the other bloodsucker terms, and is most often applied to the flickering specks of insect life hovering about in the gloaming or capturing glints of sunlight above water. Thomas Hardy evokes a slightly more benign scene in *Tess of the d'Urbervilles* (1891), capturing the moment of the setting sun's slanting rays when 'Gnats, knowing nothing of their brief glorification, wandered across the shimmer of this pathway, irradiated as if they bore fire.' Likewise, Dickens uses the imagery of 'a thousand gossamer gnats' as dusk falls in *A Tale of Two Cities* (1859), and in *Martin Chuzzlewit* (1844) contrasts 'the bee . . . humming of the work he [sic] had to do' with 'the idle gnats, forever going round and round in one contracting and expanding ring'. Gnat was also the regular term of choice for William Shakespeare, who used them to evoke a sense of hazy days, rising thermals and slanting evening light: 'When the sun shines, let foolish gnats make sport' (*The Comedy of Errors*, c. 1594), 'Whither fly the gnats but to the sun' (*Henry VI*, Part 3, 1595), and 'Is the sun dimm'd that gnats do fly in it?' (*Titus Andronicus*, 1594).

'Gnats' and 'midges' are still flying, although these terms are slightly tainted with archaism. 'Mosquito', on the other hand, is a name very much of the moment; a modern word, with more

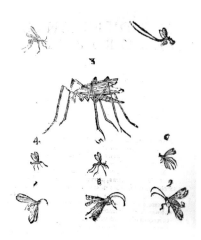

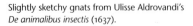

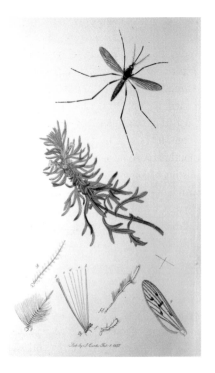

Slightly sketchy gnats from Ulisse Aldrovandi's
De animalibus insectis (1637).

Culex guttatus, the white-spotted gnat or
mosquito, from John Curtis, *British Entomology*,
vol. VIII (1839). Curtis sold his *British Entomology*
to subscribers in parts issued every few weeks.
His sales, even of disreputable creatures like
mosquitoes, relied on exquisite engraving skills.

precise scientific meaning and portent. The word derives from the
Spanish and Portuguese diminutive of *mosca*, or fly (Latin *musca*
again), and is a much more modern construct (1583, according to
the *Oxford English Dictionary*). Musket, originally a crossbow firing
stinging bolts, then a hand-held gun, appeared from the same
root around the same time (1587). It's tempting to suggest that
this is no accident, but fits precisely with the imperial aspirations
and moves of the major European powers, out to mosquito-
infested south Asia, Africa and the New World at exactly this time,
exchanging important words as increasing trade, competition,
conflict and conquest brought them closer together.

Today, the word 'mosquito' is technically applied by entomologists to just one family of midge/gnat biting flies, the Culicidae – from the Latin *culex*, one of those several words widely used in ancient writings to signify a biting gnat. Mosquitoes are distinguished from similar long-legged and long-winged relatives by a combination of the particular structure of their bloodsucking mouthparts, some distinctive wing vein patterns, the microscopic dusting of sometimes prettily arranged scales on body, legs and wings, and a fringe of long scales along the trailing edges of the wings. Under the microscope, mosquitoes are often revealed as delicately painted masterpieces of biological creation. Some, like the bizarrely foot-tufted *Sabethes belisarioi*, are truly exquisite in colour and startling in form.

If it were not for their unpleasant biting habits, mosquitoes might well have been chosen by early naturalists (very often members of the clergy and wealthy gentlemen of leisure) seeking instruction and wonder in the designs of God and wanting to fill their cabinets of curiosity with beautiful objects. Instead,

Anatomically suspect gnats, 1763. Until the regular use of the microscope, general confusion of gnats, midges and other biting bugs was widespread, as was any clear understanding of their structure.

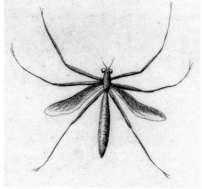

brightly coloured beetles and butterflies became the major focus of their inquisitive entomological minds. The lack of admiring interest in gnats and midges did nothing to dispel the general derision heaped upon them. And, although they were well known for their biting habits and their spectacular (almost supernatural) transformation from watery larva to aerial adult, a true appreciation of their diversity had to wait until the 1890s.

The first human–mosquito contacts are now lost in the fogs of prehistory. However, it is certain that mosquitoes started to appear long before there were any humans. As with all insects, their fragile, easily digested, easily destroyed bodies mean that

The North American Tlingit craftsman who made this 'mosquito' mask around 1840 imagined a bird-like beak for the insect's proboscis.

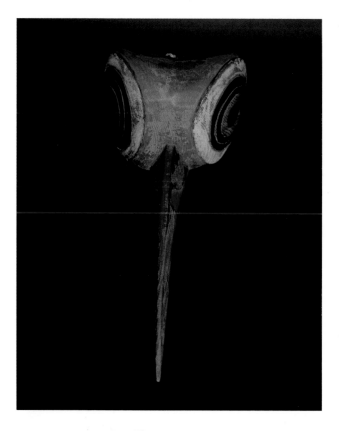

A North American Kwakwaka'wakw mosquito mask.

the mosquito fossil record is far from complete. However, beautifully preserved remains have long been known. In his treatise on natural theology, *The Wisdom of God Manifested in the Works of Creation* (1691), the prominent English naturalist John Ray considers:

> diaphanous fossils [ambers] preserved in the cabinets of the great duke of Tuscany . . . and other repositories . . . of

the admirable diversity of bodies included and naturally imprisoned with them, as flies, spiders, locusts, bees, pismires [ants], gnats . . .[6]

At the time, the nature of amber as fossilized tree sap was not fully understood, but Ray appreciated that these tiny insects, together with seeds, hair and drops of liquor, proved that it had 'been once in a state of fluidity'.

At present (2011), the oldest fossil mosquitoes we know are *Paleoculicis minutus*, trapped in Cretaceous Canadian amber 79.5–76.5 million years ago, and *Burmaculex antiquus* in mid-Cretaceous Burmese amber, from 100–90 million years ago.[7] Both are distinctly different, in some of their minute body structures, from all known modern and previous fossil mosquitoes, but they share the key characters of wing venation, scale patterns and mouthparts, and so they are, indeed, truly mosquitoes. Most important, the mouthparts are well preserved in both specimens and it is clear from their forms that they were adapted for drinking vertebrate blood.

It is now reckoned that mosquitoes evolved much earlier than 100 million years ago. A non-biting sister group of tiny flies, the Chaoboridae (sometimes called phantom midges), are more widely known, from abundant fossils up to 187 million years old, so it is likely that mosquitoes appeared at least as early as this. This suggestion is reinforced by using the complex techniques of protein molecular analysis (similar to DNA sequencing).[8] By examining the cocktails of specialist blood-digesting enzymes found in modern mosquitoes, scientists have extrapolated evolution backwards. They can show that Old World and New World species started to evolve along separate genealogical lines about 95 million years ago, concomitant with the break-up of Gondwanaland into modern continents,

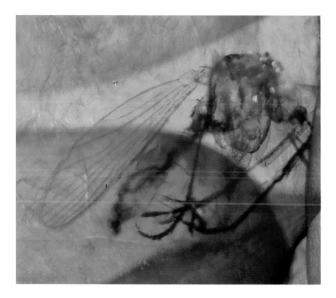

Paleoculicis minutus, trapped in Canadian amber for about 80 million years. Even then, mosquitoes had vertebrate-piercing mouthparts to suck warm red blood.

and that the main lineages of today's mosquito species started to diverge at least 150 million years ago. A general precursory bloodsucking mosquito-like group must have been present long before this.

These primeval mosquitoes were already adapted to vertebrate bloodsucking, and, though scant, their fossils occur alongside well-preserved remains of birds, primitive mammals, marsupials, lizards, snakes, turtles, crocodilians and dinosaurs, prompting the question as to what hosts they were feeding on. In his science fiction novel *Jurassic Park* (1990), Michael Crichton gave an answer: they were drinking dinosaur blood. In his successful book, DNA was extracted from host blood in the guts of amber-bound mosquitoes, and used to genetically engineer new living dinosaurs, which then roam the eponymous prehistoric theme park for paying visitors to gawp at.

The scientific possibility of extracting and sequencing blood DNA from fossilized mosquitoes remains a fiction, but Crichton's idea is based in a reality becoming more and more true as time (and technology) advances. DNA and protein sequencing have already been used on the host blood collected from the guts of living mosquitoes, enabling researchers to confirm what types of animals (including humans) they have been feeding on, and even to identify the different species of mammals and birds from which the blood meals were taken. There have been suggestions that forensic science might make use of this technique, in seeking to identify a criminal or link someone to a crime scene, by identifying their blood in the digestive tract of a mosquito found nearby. This process has already begun, and in 2005 the technique was used to aid a Sicilian murder investigation.[9]

Today there are approximately 3,500 mosquito species known from around the globe; these are variously described and classified in the scientific literature of learned journals and monographs, and with reference specimens in the world's museums. New species are being described all the time, as entomologists continue to explore the deep tropics. And, although this is not the place to go into too much detail, it is important to give a few details of mosquito classification, because different mosquitoes have had gravely different effects on human history.

Mosquitoes belong to the fly family Culicidae, which itself is divided into three subfamily units. The Toxorhynchitinae, with about 80 species in the single genus *Toxorhynchites*, are large (about 19 mm/¾ in long, with a 24-mm/1-in wingspan) and often brightly coloured in metallic blue or green with tufts of red or white scales projecting from their tail ends. They get their name from *toxon* (the Greek τοξον, for bow or archer) and *rhungchos* (ρύγχος, snout), because their large, pointed mouthparts are strongly curved backwards in a characteristic

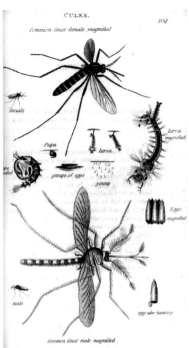

bow shape. Some authors have suggested *toxo* comes from toxa (Greek τοξα or 'arrow'), but this is more likely a projection of the idea that mosquitoes must have sharp beaks. However, the curved proboscis of *Toxorhynchites* is useless for bloodsucking: it cannot pierce skin, and these giant mosquitoes, ferocious though they may look, do not bite. Instead, they drink only nectar and other plant-liquid secretions. Consequently, they are of no medical importance and are relatively poorly studied.

The Anophelinae, with roughly 450 species in three genera, most of them in the large genus *Anopheles*, are definitely bloodsuckers. *Anopheles* species occur worldwide, and some of the

By 1758 the Dutch microscopist Jan Swammerdam had a clear understanding of insect anatomy.

Under the microscope less than 50 years later, in 1806, the fine details of the immature and adult stages of mosquitoes are becoming clearer.

The Mosquitoes' Parade, 1900, a piece for piano by Howard Whitney. With their beaked bird-like faces these mosquitoes look positively benign, probably a deliberate ploy by the publishers.

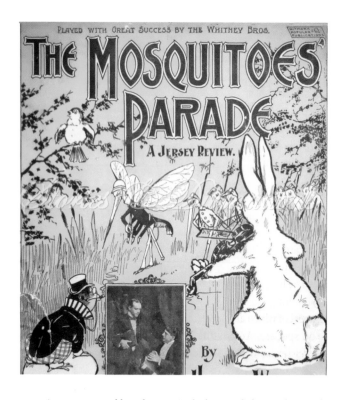

most important and best known include *Anopheles gambiae* and *An. funestus* in Africa, *An. maculipennis* in Europe, *An. freeborni* and *An. quadrimaculatus* in North America, and *An. culicifacies* in India and the Middle East. Identification guides, usually intended for experts examining pinned or pickled museum specimens, point out that *Anopheles* mosquitoes have long palps (thin feelers attached to the mouthparts), often spotted or speckled wings (caused by block arrangements of dark-coloured scales), only a single sperm-storage organ in the female abdomen, and a short-ened middle lobe of the salivary glands. The most distinctive feature in living adults is the 45-degree head-down, tail-up pose they adopt, both when resting and when supping blood. It is this unusual angular resting position that has proved to be one of the most significant messages to get across to the public, and it is highlighted again and again on warning posters and in medical pamphlets.

There is something almost balletic about this stance, emphasized by the long back legs held out into the air. The Israeli artist Miri Chais uses this characteristic pose to create a series of delicate acrylic desktop mosquito sculptures. Each comes complete with interchangeable wing patterns featuring, among other designs, atomic and molecular symbols, the nuclear disarmament ('ban the bomb') logo and a portrait of disgraced us stockbroker Bernard Madoff (perhaps being portrayed as a bloodsucker) surmounted by pigs and the slogan 'In God we trust'.

The largest mosquito subfamily, by far, is the Culicinae, with something approaching 3,000 species in about 35 genera, the largest of which are *Aedes* (about 1,000 species) and *Culex* (about 800 species). Among the better-known species, the vexatious *Aedes vexans* occurs worldwide in subtropical and temperate zones and *Ae. aegypti* is a global tropical species, while *Ae. africanus* is African and *Ae. albopictus* Southeast Asian. *Culex pipiens* is completely cosmopolitan, occurring throughout the globe, *C. quinquefasciatus* is pan-tropical and *C. tarsalis* North American. Again, those monographs and identification guides concentrate on abstruse characters like the short palps (at least in the females), less speckled and more evenly dusky wings, two or three abdominal sperm-storage sacs in the female, and the long middle lobe of the salivary glands. But the most easily spotted sign of a culicine mosquito is its body stance – strongly contrasting with *Anopheles*, it sits parallel to the surface on which it is resting or the skin through which it is biting. When

Russian artist Valery Chaliy created a huge metal mosquito sculpture from salvaged car and bulldozer parts, it was the culicines from the local quagmires of Noyabrsk that provided the threatening inspiration.

Made of salvaged car parts, the Russian mosquito statue by Valery Chaliy was inspired by the local *Culex* mosquitoes, which hold their bodies parallel to the surface on which they are resting or biting.

Today, the naming of insects (indeed all animals and plants) is governed by complex codes of scientific agreement, and great time and effort is expended on making sure that names are not muddled or duplicated. New species are constantly being discovered and named by entomologists. This is no mere counting and numbering process, and naming a new species is often given the same care as naming a child. The rules for making scientific names are dictated by certain basic conventions of Latin and Greek grammar, the need to avoid offence and frivolity, and particularly the avoidance of names already in use. Once these

A mosquito cuddly toy. A strange reversal, perhaps, in which the human child becomes the biter and chewer, rather than the bitten?

are grasped, entomologists are ever-ready to rise to the challenge of producing new names with creativity and wit. A very brief survey of mosquito names provides us with: *Aedes condolescens*, *Ae. excrucians*, *Ae. intrudens*, *Ae. insolens*, *Ae. irritans*, *Ae. lugubris*, *Ae. tormentor*, *Ae. vexans*, *Anopheles atropos* (Atropos was one of the three life-taking Fates in Greek mythology), *An. hectoris*, *Culex abominator*, *C. horridus*, *C. inadmirabilis*, *C. mortisans*, *C. perfidiosus*, *C. sphinx* (after the winged monster of Greek mythology), *Haemagogus lucifer* and *Phoniomyia diabolica*.[10]

The prominence of mosquitoes, a relatively small group among a horde of other two-winged bloodsuckers, appeared, crystallized almost, as a detailed understanding of their life history and ecology arose, and as their associations with disease were unravelled. Where once a gnat or midge was any small, annoying speck of animated malignant life, to be swatted, cursed or stoically tolerated, ever-finer distinctions between the different types became necessary to deal with the medical and biological impacts these irritating insects would have on humanity. These distinctions were not merely the preserve of specialist entomologists; they became vital tools in the work of the propagandists charged with informing the general public about mosquito dangers, and eradicating the mosquito menace which plagued not just our persons, but our very civilization.

2 Why Drink Blood?

There is something so light and airy about mosquitoes, with their narrow wings and the stilt-like gantry of their legs, that the notion of them digging deep into relatively thick and tough human skin to suck out blood seems altogether absurd. It is patently obvious that mosquitoes do bite, but why, and how, are questions intimately linked to an understanding of the complex human–bloodsucker ecology that has evolved. Ultimately, it is the why and how that has shaped the disease importance of mosquitoes.

The human body fights blood loss through the anti-trauma strategies of vasoconstriction (narrowing of the blood vessels) and clotting, because blood is, quite literally, vital to our existence. So, too, others try to extract it for their own ends. This battle between host and blood-thieves has escalated through evolutionary history and the arms race between mosquito aggressor and human defender has given rise to all the physiological and behavioural properties that make mosquitoes so important today.

In the vertebrate body, blood is transport. To use a well-worn metaphor, the arteries, veins and capillaries through which it flows are the highways and byways down which gases, nutrients and bodily products are carried. Blood has two key properties that make it such a useful and versatile bodily substance: it is a mobile fluid (human blood is about 50 per cent water) and it is rich in proteins – complex, specialized biochemicals that carry nutrients and carbon dioxide in blood serum (the fluid part) or that make up the haemoglobin in the oxygen-carrying red blood cells. These special qualities also make it highly sought-after by bloodsucking insects.

Protein richness is blood's major attraction. Protein is usually the limiting factor to growth in an animal. Herbivores spend all day chewing or grazing to extract the precious protein from vast quantities of cellulose and carbohydrate. Predation (usually hunting other insects) has evolved in all the major insect groups, because it is a much easier way of getting hold of protein. It comes at a price though – hunting each other is dangerous and prey is liable to fight back, with potentially damaging or fatal consequences. Vertebrate protein is readily targeted by insects; they scavenge vertebrate carrion or fallen antlers, nibble on fur and feathers moulted in nests, or suck blood from living vertebrates.

Strictly, mosquitoes are not solely blood-feeders, because like all insects they do virtually all of their feeding, and certainly all of their growing, as larvae; just like other insects, they manage to derive enough protein during this stage for metamorphosis into adulthood. It is the adults that then suck the blood. But this late-taken food is no mere energy-giving fuel for flight and other daily activities – that is provided by plant nectar. Incidentally, the flower-visiting habits of mosquitoes are often unappreciated, though in Canada *Aedes nigripes* is well known as a pollinator of arctic orchids.[1] Instead, there is a vital growth stage that the blood nourishes, even though the flies' bodily growing may have stopped: the growth and maturation of mosquito eggs. A very few mosquitoes, the Toxorhynchitinae for example, with their non-biting, curved mouthparts, lay eggs without a blood meal, a situation called autogenous development. They derive all the necessary nutrition for egg laying during their protein-enhanced larvahood, when they eat other mosquito larvae. This is a perfectly good way of acquiring protein, although there are always the associated risks of a predatory lifestyle. Most mosquitoes, though, go through an-autogenous development, and cannot lay eggs unless they have that vitally important vertebrate blood meal. It is as if they take a nutritional gamble; they get through the larval stage quickly and easily (without the risks associated with being a predator), but defer full egg-laying ability until they have had a nutritional top-up from vertebrate blood.

Small insects biting large vertebrates brings its own problems of size inequality, but dangerous head-to-head face-offs are avoided by adopting the sneak-attack approach that pinches just an inconsequential drop of blood. Except that it is usually not a drop of blood, it is a suck, because blood's flowing dynamics make it ideally suited to tubular sucking mouthparts rather than chewing jaws.

THE MECHANICS OF SUCKING

The roll call of bloodsucking insects testifies to blood's excellent suitability as potent nourishment. Indeed, haematophagy (feeding on blood) has appeared in insects on at least 21 separate occasions through ancient evolutionary history: lice, bugs (bedbugs and three other groups), fleas, flies (mosquitoes and thirteen other groups) and in *Calyptra*, a small genus of dull brown moths. All of these insects have stabbing and sucking mouths.

The insertion of the mosquito's snout into human skin is a delicate operation. What seems already an impossibly thin beak is mostly protective sheath, surrounding the inner stylet lance

The device that does the biting. A gnat tongue from Jabez Hogg, *The Microscope* (1854).

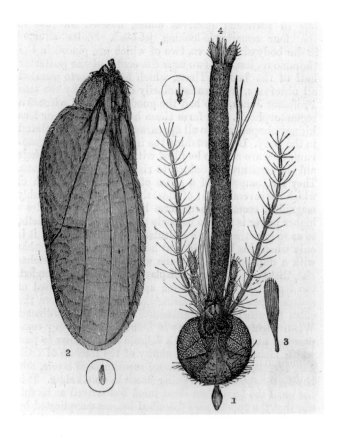

that does the penetrating. With the advent of good light microscopes in the nineteenth century, structures like the mosquito proboscis were revealed to an awe-inspired populace, rivalling the engineering marvels of the age. In 1854, the wonderfully named Jabez Hogg wrote *The Microscope: Its History, Construction, and Application*. Many such titles appeared around this time, but Hogg's tome is particularly noteworthy for its size (500–800 pages dependent on the edition), its longevity (over 30 years in print) and its equally Dickensian-sounding illustrator, Tuffen West. Accompanying one of West's excellent engravings of a mosquito head, Hogg pontificates:

> The sting of the gnat (*Culex pipiens*) is well known; although the insects themselves, so very rapid in their movements, are so much dreaded that very few people care to examine the *delicacy* and *elegance* of their *forms*. The sting is very *curiously contrived* . . . and inclosed [sic] in a sheath, folds up after one or more of the six lancets have pierced the flesh.[2]

Leaving aside Hogg's confusion of biting and stinging, his choice of words (my italics) clearly indicates a reverential wonder, even, for this despicable, bloodsucking device. West's accurate illustration, and Hogg's careful description, are as valid today as a century and a half ago. Those sheathed lancets have evolved from primitive appendages possessed by the ancestral arthropods that gave rise to all modern insects, and although wholly dissimilar in form and function, the various dissected parts can be identified and compared to the biting and chewing jaws in other insect groups.

As the mosquito pushes its mouthparts into the skin, the sheath splits open at the front and folds backwards, allowing the penetrating parts to slice down into the flesh. This needle weapon is not a simple dart, but is made up, as Hogg notes, of six interlocking rapier blades. Four of these (two mandibles and two maxillae, in entomological jargon) are sawtoothed at their tips and it is by rapid, back-and-forth movement of these that the mosquito digs through the dermis. One of the inner blades, the hypopharynx, has a narrow tube running down it, through which lubricating saliva is injected. The final, most important,

The Victorian delight in the wonders of nature fully extended to the surgical precision of the mosquito's dastardly biting equipment.

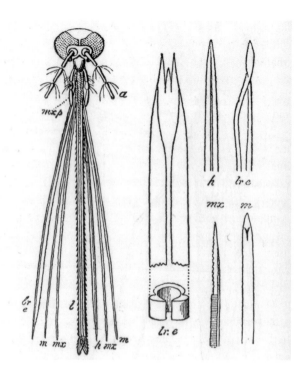

mouthpart is the hollow labrum, the straw-like tongue at the centre, through which the blood is sucked up.

Sucking human blood is not as easy as it might seem. It's certainly a lot more complicated than the Disney/Pixar movie version in *A Bug's Life* (1998), where the tipsy mosquito orders 'Hey bartender! Bloody Mary, O-positive' and is presented with a huge red glistening droplet, which he drinks down in one suck through his long, pointed nose before collapsing, comatose, on the floor.

Even without a full medical understanding, everyone has heard of blood pressure. There may be some mystery behind the exact workings of the sphygmomanometer, the tight arm-cuff device pumped up by the physician, or confusion as to what the millimetres of mercury actually represent, but there is a general awareness that the blood is pumped by a muscular heart, and that it courses, under mains pressure, through veins and arteries.

At first, it may seem foolish for such a tiny insect to attack the high-pressure blood system of a being roughly 100 million times bigger than itself. This certainly gives rise to some odd expectations, perhaps best represented by Gary Larson's cartoon in which two mosquitoes have landed for lunch and one is inflated like a balloon. 'Pull out, Betty! Pull out! . . . You've hit an artery!' implores the other. It's a nice touch that Larson uses a woman's name for his six-legged blood-pressure victim, given that, of course, only female (egg-producing) mosquitoes suck blood.

One of the first problems a hungry mosquito has to contend with is not blood pressure, but blood clotting. A tiny pinprick to the skin will draw a relatively large scarlet droplet. But the cut does not stay open for long. A physiological cascade of bio-chemical reactions quickly seals the hurt with a clot. Human blood-clotting mechanisms are complex, but because of their medical importance, they are well studied. At its simplest, damage to even the smallest capillary in the skin exposes signal proteins (notably von Willebrand factor) to the blood. These recruit clotting chemicals circulating in the blood serum, particularly collagen (a large protein molecule) and the science-fiction-sounding 'factor VIII'. At the scene of the damaged blood vessel, collagen fibres start to clog the wound, and tiny, circulating blood cells called platelets bind to them, in their turn releasing stored granules of further signal chemicals to activate more platelets. The combination of platelet bricks and collagen mortar easily and quickly seals the leak. And it is quick – initiated in a fraction of a second.

With all its digging and cutting (it may take several deep probes to find a suitable blood capillary), the mosquito's bite is, surprisingly, far from a neat hypodermic needle insertion. Tiny though the wound may be, the multiple sawing and stabbing is enough to set off the human body's clot reflexes, and, by all events, the labrum sucking tube ought to be quickly blocked by the usual crowding platelet clumps. Mosquitoes are ahead of this defence though. The injected saliva contains an anti-clotting chemical to usurp the platelet tumble. The blood flows free.

The unwary victim does not usually notice the stab. Mosquitoes have evolved to get in quickly, take a small meal, and escape. The ideal time seems to be between 2½ and 3 minutes – any less and the blood meal is not worth the risk taken by the mosquito; any more and the pain of the drill is likely to be registered by the victim, with fatal results for the insect.[3] During this typical 2½ - to 3-minute mealtime, the female mosquito sucks up a stomachful of blood. This is not a passive filling,

The vampire slayer versus the mosquitoes, from *Mosquito* by Dan James (2005). It would be unfair to prospective readers to give away the book's ending; let's just say that in this case, the mosquitoes do not get swatted.

powered by the host's blood pressure, but an active sucking, expedited by two muscular pumps, one in the head, one in the thorax. As the mosquito feeds, her abdomen expands and her previously slim grey body becomes an ominously bloated translucent red.

VAMPIRE BUGS

There is something primordially unnerving about blood-sucking creatures. Human history is littered with dark tales of vampirism and ceremonial blood drinking. The gothic horror genre is well populated with vampire bats, werewolves and other bloodthirsty human/animal intermediates. In the real world, there is a natural revulsion associated with fleas, lice, leeches and various other parasites that feed on human blood. Part of this is, no doubt, through association with filth, disease and danger (real or imagined), and part must be an innate resistance to being eaten alive. Except when populating teen romance novels, creatures that drink human blood are universally reviled. It is no surprise that some of this unease gets passed on to mosquitoes.

Heavy rock band Pearl Jam seem to accept their sated 'Red Mosquito' with a stoic fatefulness. They blame the Devil for the mosquito's bites. The stolen drop of blood that colours the fly, now bright red, is just a cunning reminder that he is out there, waiting, and the punctures in the neck are his way of letting you know he's hovering just out of sight. Similarly, Californian band Queens of the Stone Age used almost cannibalistic overtones in their 'Mosquito Song'. First, the mosquitoes come to suck blood until all that's left is skin and bone. Then, after references to being bitten on feet and legs comes imagery of butchery and cookery. Eventually, it is not clear who is eating whom alive. Is it the mosquitoes? Or the dark narrator? Whichever, the song ends with a fine summary of human blood availability – to them, we're all just living food.

This vampirish, walking food aspect of mosquito hunger is also part of the murky, simmering gloom of John Updike's poem, 'Mosquito':

I was to her a fragrant lake of blood
From which she had to sip a drop or die
A reservoir, a lavish field of food[4]

One vampire book that features the flies is the fairly obviously titled *Mosquito*, by Dan James.[5] This curious but beguiling, wordless graphic novel follows the journey of a vampire-hunting explorer who is sent money, a map and Polaroid pictures of dead bodies from South America. Not knowing if this is a hoax or a mystery, he sets out to destroy the beast. At one point he is bitten by mosquitoes, and a final twist involves the vampire sucking out the blood from the mosquitoes, before releasing them again.

On a slightly lighter note, Bill Waterson's cartoon six-year-old, Calvin, was right to run away from mosquitoes, even if overwrought and confused as he screams: 'Vampire bugs! Run for your life!'

Blood is imbued with great significance across many human cultures. Various religious groups, notably Jehovah's Witnesses, refuse to accept blood transfusions as this is, to them, analogous to eating blood, a nutrient expressly forbidden by the Bible. Terms like blood brother, blood relative, bloodline, blood money and bloodthirsty carry weight well beyond the biological measure of a red bodily fluid, and hark back to a time when blood was seen as the very liquor of life. It should really be no surprise

The translucent body of the mosquito reveals its stolen blood cargo.

that humans are wary of any animal, whether vampire bat or mosquito, trying to steal it.

JUST A PINPRICK

The mosquito takes only a minuscule volume of blood. It is not even a drop, merely a tiny bit of a drop. A large mosquito will usually imbibe 1–5 mg, that's 1–5 thousandths of a ml (1–5 thousandths of around 0.034 fl. oz), although up to 8 mg is recorded.[6] For an adult human, with about 5 l (1.3 US gal./1 imp. gal.) of blood flowing through his or her body, this is roughly 1–5 five-millionths of total blood volume; a truly trivial amount. In his short poem 'The Mosquito Knows', D. H. Lawrence neatly sums this up:

39

The mosquito knows full well, small as he is
he's a beast of prey.
But after all
he only takes his bellyful,
he doesn't put my blood in the bank.[7]

We can, perhaps, forgive Lawrence for not realizing that only shes rather than hes will be taking the bellyfuls.

It may only be a few five-millionths of our blood volume that is taken, but anyone who has been bitten by a mosquito, and then vengefully struck it down, will have noticed the dramatic discrepancy between the apparently tiny body of the living insect and the large smear of blood its remains leave behind. D. H. Lawrence returned to the subject of mosquitoes to write his beautiful masterpiece of evocative poetry, called simply 'The Mosquito'. It starts with the poet's thoughts on the fly's long legs and secret mode of attack:

What do you stand on such high legs for?
Why this length of shredded shank?
You exaltation?

Is it so that you shall lift your centre of gravity upwards
And weigh no more than air as you alight on me,
Stand upon me weightless, you phantom?

And, after the unequal combat, it finishes with the surprise:

Queer, what a big stain my sucked blood makes
Beside the infinitesimal faint smear of you!
Queer, what a dim dark smudge you have
    disappeared into![8]

Yes, it is surprising, and slightly disturbing, what 1–5 mg (about 0.000035–0.000176 oz) of blood looks like. It was deliberately meant to disturb passers-by who noticed smeared red blobs splashed across illuminated adverts along the main streets of Atlanta, Georgia in the summer of 2010. It looks as if real mosquitoes have crashed into the brightly lit billboards, and fake wings carefully cut out from fine netting are stuck down amidst the splashes. The artist (or prankster) is unknown, but images and awareness spread on an appreciative internet. Part of the uneasiness about squashing a full mosquito is the fact that it is our own blood we are smearing. American writer and poet Brad Leithauser puts it very aptly:

The lady whines then dines, is slapped and killed
Yet it's her killer's blood that has been spilled.[9]

Distasteful as the swatted mosquito and its spilled blood cargo may be, the blood loss itself is virtually nothing to the human victim. What *is* noticed, however, is the painful red bump that appears a few minutes after the bite. The lump, sometimes several centimetres across in susceptible people, is not caused by the removal of that infinitesimal amount of blood, but by an allergic reaction – the body's immune system responding to the injected mosquito saliva, with its cocktail of anticoagulants. It is this welt that is often more annoying than the bite itself. Like all lumps and bumps on the skin, the exact size depends on individual reactions, and individual vanity. It's not uncommon to hear claims of mosquito bites the size of ping-pong balls or that someone had been bitten so many times their skin looks like bubble wrap.

In the end, it is not the frustration and annoyance at a single bite that vexes most mosquito victims, it is the feeling of persistent, dogged attack from skin-crawling hordes. It was these multiple attacks that first lifted mosquitoes beyond being simply irritating trifles, and raised them to the level of infuriating, noxious pests.

3 Pest Proportions

Whoever came up with the expression 'the attention span of a gnat' was definitely not a victim of mosquito-biting. One of the most unnerving aspects of mosquito behaviour is their dogged persistence. Humans live in a world where sight is the dominant sense, and we may assume that we are safer if we stay indoors, keep a low profile or wear sensible clothes. Unfortunately, we smell, and mosquitoes hunt us by the scents we give off.

It has long been known that mosquitoes are attracted to carbon dioxide in our breath. This is a 'long-distance' hunting technique, useful over scores or hundreds of metres. The mosquitoes find the source of the carbon dioxide by flying upwind. If they lose the scent, they just drift downwind a bit, or move crosswind, left or right, until they pick up the plume again.

Perhaps the most striking feature of their carbon dioxide detection is that mosquitoes ignore a continuous concentration of the gas, even if it is raised above normal background levels. They are not attracted to continuous emitters like fires or decomposing organic matter. They are, however, highly stimulated by pulses of carbon dioxide – pulses caused, very conveniently, by breathing.

Mosquitoes can also detect 'odorants' in our perspiration. The thirteenth-century encyclopaedist Albert von Bollstädt, usually known as Albertus Magnus, was paraphrasing Aristotle

The mosquito comes to symbolize irritating distraction and painful loss of sleep in a seedy hotel in the Coen Brothers' black comedy *Barton Fink* (1991).

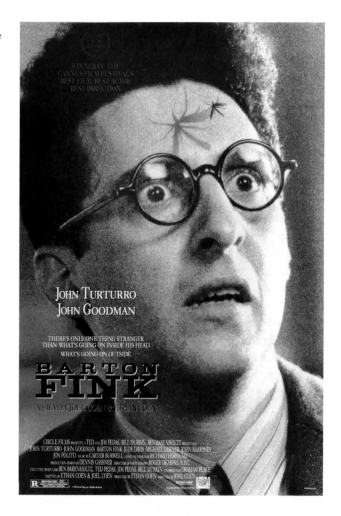

when he wrote in his *De Animalibus*: 'They have a predilection for men and animals that sweat and therefore they are found much on sleeping persons.'[1] Many folk repellents are based on the notion that these odours can be masked; Aristophanes suggested vinegar, hemp, onion and burned shells.[2] Unfortunately, mosquitoes are attracted to specific substances, rather than just body odour. These simple chemicals occur in such minute amounts that we are completely unaware of them ourselves. Chief among these seems to be nonanal (nonanaldehyde), a nine-carbon aldehyde that, concentrated in a bottle, smells like fruit or flowers. Combined with carbon dioxide, nonanal sets mosquito antennae aquiver.[3] This is their target-acquired signal; the mosquito can, quite literally, smell its next meal, and it won't give up.

Associating mosquitoes with night-time darkness is deep-seated, and is often exploited by writers wanting to juxtapose the calm rest of sleep with something more tense. Although it did not make it into the current edition of Tintin's adventures, Hergé used such a device in the original black-and-white strips of *The Broken Ear*, serialized in *Le Petit Vingtième* from 1935–7. While sleeping, Tintin dreams he is being stalked by a South American native who fires a dart at him using a blowpipe. He awakes to find that he has, instead, been bitten by a mosquito.

An altogether more sinister air is conjured up in the opening credits to the US TV police drama *Dexter* (2006–present). The title sequence starts with a mosquito on the arm of the series lead, Dexter Morgan, played by Michael C. Hall; it sinks its proboscis into his sleeping flesh, but in a sudden slap, he flattens it into a bloody splat. The sequence continues with him nicking himself shaving, splashing tomato ketchup over his bacon and eggs, and then messily squeezing the dark juice from a blood orange. There are red stains everywhere. This is, of course, significant, because Dexter is an expert on blood splatters (a 'bloodstain pattern analyst') with the Miami Police.

But not all mosquitoes bite at night. In fact, determining when and where they are active has been one of the main strands of mosquito research for over 100 years. In central Africa, the notorious *Coquillettidia fuscopennata* starts feeding just after sundown, and bites through the night. At sun-up, the equally infamous *Aedes aegypti* takes over. There is a similar spectrum of mosquito preferences when it comes to flying height. In the Mamirimiri Forest of Uganda, *Anopheles gambiae* flies near ground level and is a constant biter of people, but *Aedes africanus* is most

A cartoon mosquito from *Bee Movie* (2007): cute and cuddly, and hardly pest-like at all.

abundant in the branches around 20 m (65 ft) up, and when it can't get human blood, it feeds on monkeys. Another key behaviour is whether a particular mosquito species seeks out dark crevices as resting places, or whether it is happy to settle under a leaf, or simply on an exposed tree trunk. This roosting behaviour determines whether a mosquito is likely to venture into the dark shelter of huts and houses (and bite the occupants indoors), or primarily remain outside and bite in the open.

Across the 3,500 mosquito species known, the diversity of feeding and breeding times, flying heights, hiding places, geographic localities and resting, roosting and biting behaviours has evolved to coincide with a broad variety of potential host behaviours. It is this ubiquity, across so many climatic, geographical and habitat lines, that has made mosquitoes so successful. In fact, there is always a mosquito around to bite.

The single bite always comes at some inconvenient moment. Right in the middle of a pregnant pause, at the height of dramatic tension, or during lunch. In their quirky post-Morrison song 'The Mosquito' (1972), The Doors bleat on about the mosquito's mealtime attentions, rhyming it with burrito. Not their best work, but indicative of how mosquitoes are always getting in the way. At least in DreamWorks' *Bee Movie* (2007) the mosquito gets its comeuppance. After the human protagonist, florist Vanessa (Renée Zellweger), first discovers that hive malcontent Barry B. Benson (Jerry Seinfeld) can talk, they have a series of bizarre 'dates'. During a restful picnic in the park, they're sitting back enjoying the moment when a mosquito lands on Vanessa. Without a thought, she slaps it dead. A moment of faux pas anxiety is frozen on her face, before both human and bee crack up laughing.

Mosquitoes are a pest for only one of these 1890s women; the other presumably used the right soap.

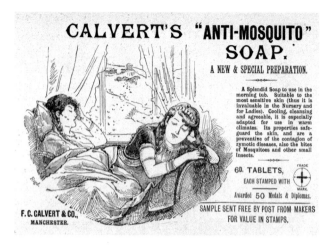

CALVERT'S "ANTI-MOSQUITO" SOAP.

A NEW & SPECIAL PREPARATION.

A Splendid Soap to use in the morning tub. Suitable to the most sensitive skin (thus it is invaluable in the Nursery and for Ladies). Cooling, cleansing and agreeable, it is especially adapted for use in warm climates. Its properties safe-guard the skin, and are a preventive of the contagion of zymotic diseases, also the bites of Mosquitoes and other small Insects.

6D. TABLETS,

EACH STAMPED WITH

Awarded 50 Medals & Diplomas.

F. C. CALVERT & CO., MANCHESTER.

SAMPLE SENT FREE BY POST FROM MAKERS FOR VALUE IN STAMPS.

MORE THAN JUST A PINPRICK

The single mosquito bite may be annoying, and that satisfying slap to kill it is at least some recompense, but the malevolence increases dramatically with greater numbers. Each mosquito only takes its 1–5 thousandths of a millilitre of blood, but it does not take many to leave a series of painful reminders of their visitations.

In some places, mosquito attack is not just from a few night-time pesterers. Clouds of insects are so thick they look like smoke, and the sucked victims, human or animal, are driven to wild distraction. At one time, there were fears that heavy mosquito attacks might cause significant blood loss, but this would be virtually impossible unless the unfortunate victim were already on the verge of anaemia.

This is not to say that multiple mosquito attack is not dangerous. There are very credible reports of dogs and cattle being literally bitten to death. In 1600, Portuguese soldier and traveller Pedro Teixeira wrote of his travels in Mexico: 'Along most of this road [Acapulco to San Juan de Ulua] is a plague of mosquitoes, so terrible and grievous that no defence avails against them; and so they stung my best slave to death for me.'[4]

There are some brave souls who, in the interests of medical science, have measured mosquito-biting rates in the field using their own bodies. The single exposed forearm of one willing victim in a Canadian swamp was attacked nearly 300 times per minute.[5] The researchers extrapolated, calculating 9,000 bites per minute for a 'totally unprotected' man. Strange and unlikely though this might be, the calculations continue, and it is reported that, in under two hours, the masochist nudist would have lost half his blood – a likely fatal outcome.

Setting aside, for the time being, diseases spread by mosquitoes, multiple bites can be dangerous, even fatal, but not through blood loss. The painful, swollen lump following a single bite is caused by an allergic reaction to the injected mosquito saliva. The human body is extremely good at recognizing even this pitifully small invasion of alien proteins, and it launches an immune counter-attack. The body's major defence is to release histamine, a biochemical that causes the local blood vessels to dilate. This increases the flow of blood, with its chemical antibodies and invasion-fighting white blood corpuscles, into the attack zone. It also causes the redness and swelling typical of bites and stings. At the extreme, the immune response to the mosquito's saliva escalates to the self-destructive overload of anaphylactic shock and the whole body reacts massively, by unnecessary and sometimes fatal mass-release of histamine and other defensive biochemicals. Anaphylactic shock in response to mosquito bites is almost unheard of (it is usually associated with bee and wasp stings). Nevertheless, multiply the mosquito's pinprick assault by many thousands and it's not surprising that

Frank Bellew's wood engraving of 'Protye's patent mosquito armour', from *Wild Oats* (1876); it keeps out the mosquitoes, but lets in other itching insects.

the body's immune system goes into hunker-down defence mode. It is likely that those cows, dogs and Teixeira's best slave died as a result of at least some over-sensitivity to mosquito saliva.

In this woodblock print by Suzuki Harunobu (*c.* 1724–1770), a girl does not leave the safety of the mosquito net whilst trying to restrain her lover from departing.

SECRETS OF FLIGHT

As we've discussed, their persistence in attack, and the painful bites they deliver, have given mosquitoes the reputation for being deliberately troublesome or vengeful. They seek out the hidden sleeper or the relaxing picnicker and are often missed until the deed of blood-letting is done. In the late 1930s, when British aviation company de Havilland was developing a stealthy fighter-bomber, Mosquito was an obvious name for it. It went on to become an icon of British aeronautical prowess, and just one of many examples of the small, bloodsucking fly giving rise to brand names where an edge of danger, annoyance or cool was required.

It is no wonder that such an acrobatic plane should be named after a fly. And it is no coincidence that flies, supreme aeronauts, are named for the very act of flying itself. Despite its flimsy body and unfeasibly long legs, the success of the mosquito as a stealthy bloodsucker is more than partly down to the fact that it has (like other flies) just two wings. Most flying insects have four wings, and there is no doubt that the ancestral insect type had this number, too. But two wings is better, and only the flies (insect order Diptera, *di-ptera* meaning two-winged) have this number, reduced long ago in evolutionary history so that what were once back wings are now little more than tiny, sensory knobs used in balance and three-dimensional orientation.

Having only a single wing on each side of the body gives flies much greater manoeuvrability, speed and stealth (the same applies to planes, of course.) Indeed, some insects – butterflies, moths, bees and wasps – couple front and back wings together with small hooks, so that the four wings operate as just two aerofoils. Lots of flies utilize their aeronautic ability to perform spectacular manoeuvres: hovering in mid-air, landing upside down on the ceiling, pouncing at top speed and skulking about in the herbage.

It is the gentle landing hover that has given mosquitoes a sneak-attack advantage when it comes to the bloodsucking battle with humans. The gentle touchdown is achieved by a combination of long, impact-absorbing legs and the structure of the wings. The narrow shape of the wings is energy-efficient and the scales, whether forming pretty patterns or an even dusting, help reduce drag. The fringes of long scales on the trailing edge of mosquito wings act like ailerons, reducing turbulence during flapping.

With small, narrow wings comes a high frequency of wingbeats. Most textbooks give 400–600 Hz (beats per second) for mosquito wings; this is towards the high end of insect flapping capability.[6] In other flying animals, flapping frequency is dictated by the maximum speed at which nerves can generate and fire impulses, then recover again for the next impulse – hummingbirds manage about 90 Hz, for example. For large insects, like dragonflies, wing speeds of this same order are adequate, but these frequencies become much too slow to sustain tiny insects. To get over this, the wings of more 'advanced' insects (like flies) are no longer stimulated by direct signals from the central nervous system. Instead, the wings self-stimulate. As the wings flap down, they distort the stiff box of the thorax, tweaking internal sensors that automatically fire internal signals to muscles that pull the wings back up; as they do so, they flex the thorax again and tweak more sensors, which fire signals to other muscles that flap the wings down again. With central nerve transmission now unnecessary, the wing stimulation/firing/flapping/recovery cycle is shortened to the point where wings can flap at over 1000 Hz. Polish entomologist Olavi Sotavalta found that the tiny biting midge, *Forcipomyia*, could vibrate its wings at 1046 Hz, but he was able to increase this to 2200 Hz by heating up the insect and cutting off most of its wings.[7] Perhaps he was exacting a childish vengeance on the bloodsucker during his experiments.

The combination of fast wingbeat and long, narrow wings gives an insect supreme aerial dexterity. It also creates its audible buzz. The high-pitched whine of a mosquito is something that most people will recognize, even without a detailed knowledge of dipteron structure or physiology. But it can be misunderstood. The ancient Greeks supposed that insects produced their buzz by an opening in the abdomen. Aristophanes claimed that 'the behind of the empides is a trumpet'.[8] In the dark silence of the night bed, a mosquito's whine is audible as the fly descends around the ears to a vulnerable neck, but only a few centimetres away, it is unheard. High-frequency wing movements, giving a high-pitched note, are surprisingly quiet compared to, say, the lower, louder buzz of the bluebottle or even the housefly. This does not stop a bit of exaggeration. US singer-songwriter and rock icon Iggy Pop sang about the mad gyrations of the 'Loco Mosquito', but it's puzzling to know what insect he was singing about. The secret to a mosquito assault is stealth, not the frenzied buzzing this energetic rock song suggests.

Of course, in cartoons, anything goes. Walt Disney's *Camping Out* (1934) sets Mickey Mouse and friends against, initially, a lone humming mosquito, then all its friends and family. The high-pitched whine of the inquisitive insect turns to full-throttle internal-combustion roar as it makes its run-up to prang the backside of Mickey's horse-friend Horace. This short film is loaded with other mosquito gags: the initial mosquito 'singing' along to the music; the angry mob taking on the silhouette of one giant mosquito; and mosquitoes' pointed beaks being dis-armed with peas, clothes pegs and clinching hammer blows. It is slightly surprising that the film shows mosquitoes in an almost sympathetic light. This is something that was to change dramatically when Disney produced *The Winged Scourge* in 1943.

The hum of the mosquito has also been interpreted in other ways. In Mayan culture, mosquitoes were spies, able to discern names and secrets from the blood of their victims, then whisper

Just one of many mosquito-based gags in the Disney short *Camping Out* (1934).

them in secret. In one traditional West African myth (lovingly retold by Verna Aardema[9]), the Mosquito lies to Iguana, who puts sticks in his ears so he cannot hear, but then does not notice Python, who gets upset and scares Rabbit, who startles Crow . . . and a trail of distress and confusion spreads through the forest, resulting in Owl refusing to hoot-up the sun in the morning. Lion oversees a tribunal to unravel the blame, and eventually everyone is appeased; Owl summons the sun, but Mosquito hides to avoid punishment. To this day, he goes about whining in people's ears: 'Zeee! Is everyone still angry at me?' Of course, he then gets swatted.

Back in the real world, mosquitoes are far quieter than might be supposed. Buzzing loudly to advertise their presence would be an evolutionary dead-end. The stealth works and by it they are very good at getting blood. Mosquitoes need the blood to produce and mature their eggs and, unless they get swatted (or, more likely, eaten by some predator or other), the eggs will be laid a few days later.

Mosquitoes lay their eggs in all sorts of water, from large rivers, lakes, ponds and marshes to small puddles, ruts and flooded tin cans. They do, however, show a marked preference for dark, stagnant, often fetid, pools, ditches, gutters and swamps. This preference has not gone unnoticed.

4 Mosquito Places

The association of mosquitoes (gnats and midges, too) with fens and swamps has been known for millennia. Herodotus, writing in the fifth century BCE, describes the marsh country of Egypt, and how the people there avoided being bitten by the *conopides*, as the sharp-faced gnats of the time were called. The Egyptians slept on raised platforms where the wind prevented the flies from settling, and they threw their fishing nets over their beds when they slept. Columella, in the first century CE, wrote that farmsteads should not be sited near marshes because it produces creatures armed with troublesome stings.[1]

Aristotle describes how such flies breed in muddy water and he links them to the group of insects that he believes are spontaneously generated from putrefaction, rather than being the progeny of a mating. He describes how the wriggling worms are generated in the mud at the bottom of wells or ponds. His now rather strange narrative suggests that the mud changes from white to black, then red, and that filaments resembling seaweed start to grow, before breaking off into free-floating red worms.[2] Giving a modern entomological explanation of these ancient writings is difficult. The word he uses for these worms – ασκαριδες, askarides – he uses elsewhere for internal parasitic worms, and it is related to words meaning both 'jump' and 'palpitate', which could refer to the skipping motion of mosquito larvae or the undulating bodies of non-biting midge larvae (family Chironomidae). Blood-red worms in aquatic mud are usually the larvae of these chironomid midges. The worms' redness comes from haemoglobin, the same red, oxygen-carrying chemical found in vertebrate blood. The midge larvae use haemoglobin to store oxygen, and they can release it in times of deficit, allowing them to live in deep-water mud where other animals cannot survive. Some confusion caused by a mix-up between 'blood' in the larvae and the blood sucked by adult mosquitoes is, perhaps, not altogether unexpected.

Writing in the thirteenth century, Albertus Magnus was reworking Aristotle when he wrote: '*Cinifes* [another variant of *conops*] are flying worms with long legs. They pierce the human skin with a small proboscis. They originate in moisture and are frequent near water.'[3]

Anglers have long known that various gnats emerged from the water, even if they did not ascribe clear scientific names to them. They gave the adults folk names and crafted fishing lures after them – in Scotland, there were blaes and blacks; in Ireland, duckflies. Ruby gnats, olive gnats and black gnats were, if not scientifically understandable, at least descriptive, and may refer to mosquitoes, biting midges and blackflies respectively.[4]

The general vagueness of slightly different aquatic worms turning into slightly different flying midges continued into the modern era. Just as 'gnat' or 'midge' was about as accurate as it got when describing the adults, 'worm' was about the only description available when it came to the larvae. Distinctions between the different groups of adult flies became ever finer as entomologists sought to classify them, particularly when the nineteenth century brought keen examination under the microscope. At the same time, their different aquatic life histories were being deciphered. Of all the wriggling worms and flying

The larva of a culicid mosquito hangs down from the water meniscus from its breathing siphon.

midges to choose, it is perhaps slightly ironic that the mosquito should be the one that was most popularly studied.

WATERY BEGINNINGS

Mosquito eggs are laid in water, often stuck together in floating rafts, and the larvae live in the water. The 'wiggler' larvae are well named for their agile writhing movements. They mainly live at the water surface, taking air through the spiracle (breathing pore) at the tail end, while sieving out microscopic food particles of decaying plant and animal matter at the mouth end. If disturbed, by a passing shadow, they dive down into the murky safety of the deeper water by vigorous flips of their narrow bodies.

Just as adult mosquito types can be identified by their resting body stance, so too can the larvae, by the angle at which they hang down into the water from the surface tension. It's all to do with how and what they are feeding on. Anopheline species (subfamily Anophelinae) rest parallel to the water surface, hanging here by a ring of water-repellent hairs around the tail-tip breathing pore and other fan-like hairs along the body. They feed by collecting minute particles of decaying organic matter from the surface, and in a strange departure from normal front/ back animal anatomy, the larva rests belly-down in the water, but rotates its head 180 degrees so its mouthparts, and the fine brushes of hair it uses to agitate the water, are pointed upwards.

Culicine species (subfamily Culicinae) hang down from the surface at an angle of about 45 degrees, suspended by a long breathing siphon. *Aedes* larvae swim about nibbling small pieces of algae, or dead leaves; others use their mouth brushes to create eddies to bring floating organic particles into the mouth. These contrasting resting positions are, very neatly, the exact opposite of the striking adult poses (Anophelinae, tail 45-degrees up in the air; Culicinae, body parallel to the surface), and the differences are used to good effect in identification charts.

With the advent of cheap microscopes, cheap printing and the Victorian enthusiasm for nature study, the transformation of the wriggling maggot into the adult fly became one of the standard wonders of nature. It was all the more astonishing because worm-like watery nymph gave rise to faerie airborne imp. Rearing caterpillars through to butterflies may have been more spectacular, but that required at least some knowledge of

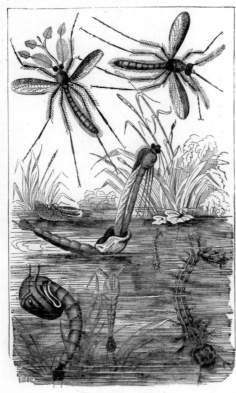

Although mosquitoes are derided as the bloodsuckers 'that murder sleep', this lovely woodcut from the children's book *Half Hours in the Tiny World* (c. 1900) demonstrates the Victorian awe that such wondrous transformations engendered.

TRANSFORMATIONS OF THE GNAT.

larval foodplants, and more than a little skill in avoiding the perennial problems of mould and premature escape. Rearing mosquitoes just needed a jam jar full of murky water.

Descriptions and diagrams of mosquito metamorphosis run through all levels of the burgeoning scientific literature of the nineteenth century. At the popular end of the scale, they suited the reverential tone of the 'juveniles', the mass-produced

Swamp as allegory in a US political cartoon of 1909: if you want to get rid of the mosquitoes (subsidized senators, lobbyists, grafters, kept congressmen, protected monopolies, etc.), you have to drain the swamp (the tariff of politics).

illustrated books for 'younger folks' printed from the 1880s onwards for increasingly literate middle-class readers. They were usually accompanied by lovely illustrations of the 'transformations of the gnat', showing, especially, the adult fly heaving its delicate body out of the fragile pupal casing. At the more academic end of the spectrum, equally careful and precise illustrations were accompanied by scientific insights into larval body segmentation, respiration, growth patterns, limb formation and hydrophobicity.

Whether lowbrow or erudite, one fact comes to the fore: mosquitoes breed where there is standing water – marshes, pools, ponds or flooded jam jars. The mosquito is inextricably linked to its watery habitat.

Despite the negative connotations, there are plenty of mosquito place names in the world. Google Maps are helpful here. At the parochial end of the spectrum, there are Mosquito Roads in West Malling (Kent), Upwood (Cambridgeshire) and in George-town and Placerville (California). There is a Mosquito Way in Hatfield (Hertfordshire) and a Mosquito Lane in Wallingford (Oxfordshire). Quite how mosquito-infested they are is not known. In a slightly less tenuous link to the flies' swamp habi-tats, there are also Mosquito Lake Road (Deming, Washington), Mosquito Creek Road (Clark Ford, Idaho) and Mosquito Brook Road (Hayward, Wisconsin). Not surprisingly, there is no grandly named Mosquito Boulevard or Mosquito Avenue in any major metropolis in the world.

Some mosquito names are, without doubt, down to the ex-hausted vexation of early cartographers and explorers, struggling through buggy swamps and across midge-blown moors. The Mosquito Range forms part of the Rockies in Central Colorado. There are Mosquito Harbours (Maine, Vancouver, Ontario), Mosquito Island (British Virgin Islands), and plenty of Mosquito Creeks (Alberta, Vancouver, California, Ohio, Victoria in Austra-lia). All of these are obvious dank mosquito habitats.

Contrary to some people's expectations that mosquitoes mainly inhabit tropical climes, it is the open, cool wastes of moor, muskeg, morass and mire which often host the greatest numbers of these biting flies. In the highly biodiverse tropical rainforests, there are so many other animals to eat mosquitoes, and so many vertebrate victims for mosquitoes to bite, that their numbers (and their attentions) are reduced. But in the fertile mosquito-breeding grounds of the northern wetlands, there are miles and miles of open, watery swamp populated by

The Mexican illustrator José Guadalupe Posada wrote *El Mosquito Americano* in 1903, using the fly as a metaphor for American tourists derided as pests, and for political, industrial and technical advisors, who bring nothing but pain and corruption.

EL MOSQUITO AMERICANO

El Mosquito Americano
Ahora acaba de llegar;
Dicen se vino á pasear
A este suelo mexicano.

Dizque el domingo embarcó
Allá en Laredo de Texas,
Y que al Saltillo llegó
Picándoles las orejas,
En la Estación á unas viejas
Que bien las hizo marchar,
Hasta las hizo sudar
Este animal inhumano;
Luego empiezan á gritar:
El Mosquito americano.

A Guanajuato marchó,
Esto es cosa de reir;
Él al centro no llegó,
Pero si estuvo en Marfil.
Ya no podrán sufrir
Tan malcriado y altanero,
Pues le picó en el trasero
A un militar veterano,
Porque es mucho, muy grosero
El Mosquito americano.

Tomó el rumbo de Irapuato
Y por Péujamo pasó;
De allí luego regresó
Por el pueblo de Uriangato,
La hacienda de Villachato
La dejó muy derrotada;
Toda la gente asustada
La encontró el vale Marisno,
Nana Emeteria gritaba:
El Mosquito americano.

Por la puerta de San Juan
Piedra Gorda y la Sandía,
Una viejecita decía:
¡Jesús, qué fiero animal!
Dígame usted Don Pascual
¿No le ha llegado el Mosquito?
Dicen que es muy chiquitito,
Y también muy inhumano;
¿Qué dice tata Pachito
El Mosquito americano?

relatively low numbers of native birds and animals. As well as hunting after carbon dioxide and nonanal, biting flies are also attracted by dark silhouettes, standing out readily against the flat, featureless landscape.[5] The upright human is soon spotted, and soon bitten. Canada, with its vast, labyrinthine mosaic of lakes, rivers and marshes (making up a quarter of the world's wetlands) makes a good claim to be the most mosquito-ridden country in the world.

There is something of a love–hate relationship between Canadians and their home-grown mosquitoes, and there is a certain rivalry between towns self-proclaiming to be mosquito capitals. Winnipeg, low-lying on the Red River Valley, makes a claim, and the mosquito is jokingly said to be the provincial bird of Manitoba. Komarno, a small town about 70 km (45 m) north of Winnipeg, is claimed to be named by Eastern European immigrants from the Ukrainian word for mosquito.

The Canadian folk-rock duo Kate and Anna McGarrigle use the mosquito as a symbol of futility in their 1976 'Complainte pour Ste Catherine'. The lament for Saint Catherine (the name of a major Montreal shopping thoroughfare and also the patron saint of single girls) likens the long-time struggle of a street hooker to twenty years of war against mosquitoes. This is a poignant reference to the clouds that descend on the marshy Quebec outlands every year.

The Lomen Brothers made their name photographing early 20th century Alaska but took time out to celebrate their local mosquitoes.

Komarno, Canada, claims to be the mosquito capital of the world, and commissioned a huge statue to promote the idea.

Indeed, Canada holds the rare distinction of being the only country in the world to offer a postage stamp celebrating a place called Mosquito. The small brown Newfoundland eight-cent stamp from 1910 shows a 'View of Mosquito'. This small town was so named in 1610, the same year that nearby Cupids became the first English settlement in Canada, and only the second in North America. The naturalist and writer Philip Gosse was plagued by mosquitoes during his residence in Newfoundland

The bistre (wood pigment) 8-cent stamp from Newfoundland commemorating the town of Mosquito, later renamed Bristol's Hope, issued in 1910.

in the 1830s. Everyone was covered with 'large white tumours attended with intolerable itching'. He was kept awake by the children crying out at night, and every day the walls of the house were covered with bloated mosquitoes, 'their abdomens distended and almost bursting with the blood they have extracted from our veins at their leisure'.[6]

By 1910, the Newfoundlanders decided it was time to change their historic settlement's name to something more aspirational. Just as the stamp was published to celebrate 300 years of Newfoundland history, the town was renamed Bristol's Hope. But there is still a Mosquito Pond behind Beach Road there, and it is unlikely that any mosquitoes took much notice of this over-late public relations exercise.

THE EXPLORER'S BANE

Exactly how or why Newfoundland's settlement got its name is not precisely known, but during this era of European expansion, mosquitoes featured regularly in the travelogues written by explorers. When Captain Cook, accompanied by naturalists Banks and Solander, first landed in New South Wales on 29 May 1770, they were greatly hindered by swathes of prickly spinifex grass and 'mosquitos [sic] that were likewise innumerable . . . made walking almost intolerable'.[7] In April 1812 eccentric naturalist and traveller Charles Waterton left the town of Stabroek to travel into the wilds of Dutch Guiana, only to find that during the day the sun would exhaust him, and at night 'mosquitoes would deprive him of every hour of sleep'.[8]

The assault of humans squelching through mosquito-infested swamps makes grim reading, and it would be easy to fill countless pages with references to swampland sufferings. But a potent focus can be brought to bear on the writings of just one particular man. Throughout his long life (1823–1913), explorer, scientist and writer Alfred Russel Wallace spent much of his time and energy considering the persecutions of these tiny, biting insects. In his many books, there is a constant commentary on how and where mosquitoes were biting. In his first major publication (*A Narrative of Travels on the Amazon and Rio Negro*, 1853), he comments, for example, that in Para 'Mosquitoes, in the low parts of the city and on shipboard, are very annoying, but on the higher grounds and in the suburbs there are none.'[9]

Not surprisingly, since he was travelling by boat through this pristine, watery wilderness, mosquitoes were always with him. As he travels into the interior of South America, he frequently complains that they 'would not allow us to sleep for some hours', 'annoyed us much in the evenings' and 'were a great torture'. On several occasions he comments, with barely hidden glee, when the mosquitoes let up for a moment. When he finally gets onto the Rio Negro, he notes: 'A great luxury of this river is the absence of mosquitoes.'[10] Lack of mosquitoes may be due to the river's water quality. It gets its name from its clear, dark appearance (contrasting with the pale, silty Amazon), caused by tannins leeching out of decaying vegetation creating transparent, tea-like water, with higher than normal acidity.

Needless to say, along other Amazonian waterways, he was pestered endlessly:

> the mosquitoes here were very annoying . . . we found them unbearable . . . they soon found their way in at the cracks and keyholes, and made us very restless and uncomfortable all the rest of the night . . . We found them more tormenting than ever, rendering it quite impossible for us to sit down to read or write after sunset.[11]

He tried everything to keep them at bay:

> The people here all use cow-dung burnt at their doors to keep away the 'praga' or plague, as they very truly call them, it being the only thing that has any effect. Having got an Indian to cook for us, we every afternoon sent him to gather a basket of this necessary article, and just before sunset we lighted an old earthen pan full of it at our bedroom door on the verandah.

Luckily, the cow dung 'gives a rather agreeable odour'.[12]

Despite his regular protestations, Wallace was no pathetic whinger; he was a hardened, independent traveller risking his life among wild animals, indigenous people and all the dangers of travel in the jungle and under sail. On 6 August 1852 he was returning across the Atlantic – a few days out from Para, on the ship *Helen* – when fire was discovered deep in the hold. Despite the crew knocking holes in the cabin floors and pouring in water, the fire spread and the whole ship was eventually engulfed.

Wallace had time to grab a few notebooks and a couple of shirts before he and the entire crew had to abandon the vessel. They spent ten days in open lifeboats, until they were picked up by a passing cargo brig bound for London. Wallace, the undaunted Indiana Jones of his day, rested up in England a year, planning his next venture, and was soon off again: to the Malay Archipelago in Southeast Asia.

This time, he made full and good use of a bed net to try and get some release from his aggressors. In Aru, an island south of New Guinea, he turned in under his mosquito curtain 'to sleep with a sense of perfect security'. Mind you, 'in the plantations, where my daily walks led me, the day-biting mosquitoes swarmed, and seemed especially to delight in attacking my poor feet'.[13] Wallace was a self-financing traveller, supplying specimens (mostly birds, butterflies and beetles) to wealthy patrons back home. He needed the evenings to prepare specimens, write up his notes and correspond with his colleagues back in Britain. His mosquito net was his only solace. At one point in his records of the trip we find Wallace outraged by the lean and hungry dogs that prowled the nights below his stilted house. They had previously destroyed several valuable bird of paradise skins 'incautiously left on my table for the night', but he saves the peak of his ire for recalling those in a Dyak's house in Borneo: 'they gnawed off the tops of my waterproof boots, ate a large piece out of an old leather game bag, besides devouring a portion of my mosquito-curtain!'[14] His exclamation mark, by the way.

Wallace also suffered from ague, a recurrent fever, which frequently wracked him during his travels. He did not, at the time, know of its link to the very same mosquitoes that so vexed him. References to ague punctuate his writings: 'One of my best Indians fell ill of fever and ague . . . On leaving Sao Gabriel I was again attacked with fever, and on arriving at Sao Joaquim

I was completely laid up.'[15] And: 'I had a slight attack of fever, and almost thought that I was still doomed to be cut off by the dread disease which had sent my brother and so many of my countrymen to graves upon a foreign shore.'[16]

It was during one of these incapacitating attacks – in early 1858 at Ternate, in the Maluku Islands, 'shivering under the cold fit of ague' – that he found time to mull over ideas about the struggle for survival in nature.[17] As soon as the fever passed, he sent his famous essay to Charles Darwin, independently suggesting the idea of evolution by natural selection, and prompting Darwin to publish their world-moving joint papers at a meeting

Portrait of *Alfred Russel Wallace*, 1862.

'Stream through the Forest' from Alfred Russel Wallace, *Travels on the Amazon and Rio Negro* (1853).

of the Linnean Society in London in July later that year.[18] Wallace did not appreciate it at the time, but the single most important concept in biological science was triggered years before by a bite from one of those irritating mosquitoes somewhere in the Amazon jungles.

Wallace used the traditional English term for this ailment, ague, but very soon a more sinister word would come into fashion. Along with the biting mosquitoes that they bred, swamps and quagmires often give off the fetid and indelicate smell of decay – methane (natural gas) and hydrogen sulphide (like rotten eggs) were by-products of the bacterial breakdown of dead leaves and other organic material in the oozy muds. Near towns and cities, marshes were wet with slow-moving water, which did not flush away sewage quite as quickly as the inhabitants might have wished. Diseases like ague became linked to the foul breath of the wind off these polluted mudflats. Victims were thought to have fallen to the dangerous miasmas wafting in from the estuaries, the bad airs, the mal'aria.

5 The Parasite Within

Malaria was a mystery. For millenia, the disease appeared to strike without rationale or logic. It affected people in different ways at different times. It often appeared as if by divine intent, then sometimes disappeared from cities, even entire countries. It was as mysterious as the fogs and vapours of the marshes it haunted and its only explanation was supernatural. Some tried supernatural means to prevent it.

In November 1709, a Norfolk vicar – 'Mr Forbes, a Scotchman' – died at his living in Rougham, near Bury St Edmunds, and the woman who laid out the body found a small silk bag, tied by a ribbon around his neck. In it was a scrap of paper 'discolour'd very yellow with sweat. I transcrib'd it in the same charectar &c words as they stood there.' The unknown writer who copied the peculiar words from the paper onto a manuscript now in the British Museum thought it might be a sign of some coded political conspiracy. It began: 'Eywm uydlab ase byw udgaa eywdgmw yw esa lbib . . .' and continued for another 41 incomprehensible words. This odd language had to wait until 1932 for antiquarian Warren R. Dawson to finally translate it.[1] It was a simple cipher in which the letters are substituted, so E=W, Y=H, W=E, M=N, and so on. Dawson had discovered a charm against ague:

When Christ saw the cross wherone he was to be crusified the Jews asked him 'art thou hafraid or hast thou an ague?' Jesus said 'I am not afraid nor have not an ague'. Whoesoever w[e]ars these words shall never be troubled with an ague. Amen. Amen. Sweet Jesus.

In a cartoon by Thomas Rowlandson, 1788, fever, represented as a frenzied beast, stands centre stage, while the blue monster of ague ensnares its victim by the fire-side. The doctor, right, writes out a prescription.

Today, we know that malaria/ague is caused by a microscopic protozoan blood parasite spread by mosquitoes. The *Plasmodium* organisms that cause the disease are many orders of magnitude bigger and more complex than simple bacteria and viruses, and their transmission is as convoluted as the disease's aetiology is mystifying. This complexity masked the precise cause of malaria throughout history, but it also left clues in the symptoms recorded by contemporary observers, in descriptions

of historical events detailed by chroniclers, and in the biological material still being examined by archaeologists today.

Written records from ancient Egypt are scant, but recent DNA evidence has suggested that, around 1323 BCE, Tutankhamun died as a result of a broken leg, exacerbated by congenital disorders and severe malaria infection.[2] In the canon of Chinese medicine, diseases translated as 'malaria' are first mentioned about 800 BCE, and are seasonally linked to the cold, wet airs of autumn. At some point, it jumped to Japan, perhaps linked with the introduction of rice paddy fields around 400 BCE. Likewise, Indian medical scholars identify malaria-like diseases around 1200 BCE. The Hindu text Atharaveda comments that fevers are common after excessive rains. It also appears to distinguish between fevers that recur on the first and third (or fourth) day – typical malaria symptoms.[3]

Ancient Greece seems to have been virtually free of the disease until about 500 BCE.[4] Invading Persians were blamed for bringing it, and in fact three fevers are described accurately enough to be identifiable as three different malarias today. At a remarkably similar time, the Roman Republic, which had been seemingly malaria-free in its early years, began to report more cases. The epidemic drove peasants from the low-lying countryside into the cities (which had at least been drained), and this disruption to the Roman economy was noted.[5] The ill winds of the marshlands were well known. Vitruvius, writing his *De Architectura* in the first century BCE, advises against building farms or settlements near marshes because of the diseases, suggesting that the morning mist becomes infected with the poisonous breath of noxious creatures, especially near stagnant water.[6] Varro, writing at about the same time, links marshes to organisms that are too small to be seen by the naked eye, and which are carried on the air.[7]

For over 11,000 years, the history of the Americas is oral and therefore vague, but both north and south continents were malaria-free when European adventurers first made contact with the native populations.[8] Other diseases like smallpox and measles were the first epidemics to ravage here. But, by the middle of the seventeenth century, malaria was well established throughout the New World, and particularly troublesome across the Caribbean.

An incident of striking exactitude happened in Mauritius. This island was uninhabited until the seventeenth century, when it was settled by the Dutch, followed by the French, then the British. It was also populated by immigrations from India, Africa and China. For over 200 years of colonization, malaria was known only from a few isolated cases, always in newly arrived immigrants who had carried the disease with them, mostly from southern India. But it never spread through the general population . . . until 1866, when a huge epidemic erupted, killing 3,700 people.[9] Malaria has been present (albeit at low levels) ever since. First, though, as with any disease, it is important to give it a name – a label.

The word 'malaria' first entered the English language around 1740 in letters written from Italy by Horace Walpole.[10] However, the physician and naturalist John MacCulloch is credited with bringing the term into widespread use, with his essay written in 1827.[11] The disease was thought to be caused by ethers, like smokes or plumes, wafting through the air. An excellent description is given in *Lloyd's Encyclopaedic Dictionary* (1895):

> ma-lär'-i-a, [Ital. *mal' aria*, for *mala aria* = bad air: *mala* (Lat. *malus*) = bad, and *aria* = air.] A morbid poison of unknown character generated in paludal or littoral districts, affecting the system through the blood often as

Malaria was often portrayed as the malingerer's disease.

DOCTOR. "Any of your boarders got the malaria?"
LANDLADY. "Malaria! If you mean lying down and sleeping and eating and grumbling and
oing to bed late and don't get up at all mornings—if that's the disease, they've all got it bad."

long as twelve months after one has been exposed to it, and exerting its deadly influence in many cases through life. Hydrophobia is the only other form of disease in which the period of incubation may be as long or longer. Malaria emanates from marshy land in a decomposed state under the influence of heat above 60°F acting on the moisture; when thoroughly drained, flooded or frozen, malaria is not generated. An elevation from 1,000 to 1,200 feet is, generally speaking, a protection against it.

Malaria causes ague, intermittent and congestive fevers, and one kind of yellow fever, marked by periodicity. The Roman Campagna and the West Coast of Africa are noted haunts of malaria and malarious fevers; and rice-fields are also well-known sources of it.

THE AGUE

In Britain, the endemic malaria was known by that other name – ague. Characterized by recurring fevers (every two or three days), shivers and aches, it was frequently attached to marshes. Written in the late 1300s, Chaucer's 'The Nun's Priest's Tale' from his *Canterbury Tales* talks of 'some ague that may be your bane'.[12] Shakespeare mentions ague in eight of his plays. Sometimes this is by allusion; in *The Tempest* (1608–13), Caliban describes the 'unwholesome fen' and curses: 'All the infections that the sun sucks up / From bogs, fens, flats, on Prosper fall'. Later, Stephano mistakes Caliban's trembling for an attack of malaria: 'This is some monster . . . who hath got, as I take it, an ague . . . He's in his fit now . . .'. Stephano offers alcohol, a popular cure for ague: 'open your mouth . . . this will shake your shaking . . . the wine in my bottle will recover him, I will help his ague . . .'. A similar play on popular knowledge is at work in *Twelfth Night* (*c*. 1601), where Sir Andrew Aguecheek (also called Agueface behind his back) is a friend of the equally daftly named Sir Toby Belch. Both are drunkards, and Aguecheek in particular is a comic fool, slow-witted and slow in speech. Ague, as well as meaning the malaria of our modern understanding, was also often a very broad term for general fever and illness, shakes and shivering – a kind of Tudor or Elizabethan man-flu. Since it was self-diagnosed and self-treated, it made the ideal affliction for anyone wanting to partake of the medicinal qualities of the bottle.

Oddly, Dr J. C. Ayer claims his ague cure contains no quinine, emphasizing its vegetable origins; the frogs and crocodiles are not impressed. The tonic probably had a high alcohol content.

AYER'S AGUE CURE

Ayer's Ague Cure is a purely vegetable bitter and powerful tonic, and is, with a positive knowledge of its effects, WARRANTED a certain cure for all malarial disorders. These disorders owe their origin to a miasmatic poison, which enters the blood through the Lungs, deranges the Liver, and causes the various forms of agues and fevers, and blood-poisoning, known as Fever and Ague, Chills and Fever, Dumb Ague, Chill Fever, "Malaria," Intermittent, Remittent, Bilious, and Typhoid Fevers.

AYER'S AGUE CURE neutralizes the malarial poison, and expels it from the system. It contains no quinine, nor any mineral ingredient; is positively safe and harmless; and never fails if used according to directions. It is an excellent remedy for Liver Complaints. *Full directions with each bottle.*

PREPARED BY

Dr. J. C. AYER & CO., Lowell, Mass.

FOR SALE BY

AYER'S AGUE CURE
IS WARRANTED TO CURE
ALL MALARIAL DISORDERS.

Prepared by
Dr. J. C. Ayer & Co., Lowell, Mass.

A cartoon from an 1881 issue of *Harper's Weekly* poked fun at a Washington health officer called Townsend after he facetiously described malaria as a 'fashionable disease'; doctors diagnosed it when faced with anything they did not understand.

Daniel Defoe, in his *Tour through the Eastern Counties of England* (1722), paints a sometimes grim picture of life, where many people have an 'Essex ague on their backs'. He recounts how the men 'seasoned to the place' always went to the uplands for a wife. They 'took the young lasses out of the wholesome and fresh air', but when they brought them 'into the marshes among the fogs and damps, there they presently changed their complexion, got an ague or two, and seldom held it above half a year, or a year at most'. He noted, in particular, that these men got through a remarkable number of wives: '5 or 6 to 15 or 16' was very frequent. One such farmer was on his 25th wife.[13]

This resignation to the pattern of disease and death is both stoical and grotesque, but shows a local acceptance of ague. Folk names echo this degree of intimacy – the Bailiff of the Marshes, Lord John's Fever and Old Johnny Axey.[14] On the whole, illness from ague may have been chronic and incapacitating, but deaths were generally rare. Nevertheless, Sir Joseph Fayrer, writing in the *Transactions of the Epidemiological Society of London* in 1881–2, tells us that we have lost two kings, a queen, a cardinal and a lord protector to malaria. Horatio Nelson reputedly suffered from ague as a boy growing up in Norfolk in the 1750s and '60s, and his strength was reduced by it.

Exact disease records are sparse. There were ague epidemics in Cambridgeshire and Lincolnshire in 1826–9 and 1857–60.[15] In 1864 a Privy Council report looked at infant mortality rates across the country and found them higher than average in fenland towns. How much of this is due to ague is not clear; the report rather unsympathetically blamed much of the high mortality rate on a large number of premature births (leading to premature death), high incidence of infant neglect and inbreeding.[16]

Everywhere, though, the ague was linked to the water. In *Great Expectations* (1861) Charles Dickens begins with Pip in the local graveyard, when he meets Magwitch, drenched and shivering, escaped from the convict hulks across the mud. 'I think you have got the ague . . . It's bad about here', says Pip, standing in front of his parents' tombstone, and those of his five infant brothers. The evocation of the malarial mud is laid on thick: 'Ours was the marsh country . . . this bleak place . . . the dark flat wilderness beyond . . . the low leaden line beyond was the river . . . the distant savage lair from which the wind was rushing was the sea.' Masterful.

In 1864 a special report on the 'quantity of ague and other malarious diseases now prevailing in the principal marsh districts of England' was commissioned by and presented to the Privy Council, but the mechanisms of infection were still tantalizingly clouded. Ague sufferers were sometimes thought to get the disease by drinking ditch water. One correspondent to

The listless effects of malaria and the misty miasma-shrouded Pontine Marshes near Rome made Antoine Auguste Ernest Hébert's name when he painted *La Malaria* around 1850.

the leading medical journal, *The Lancet*, suggested changing the name malaria to mal'aqua.

When Jim Hawkins, Long John Silver and the crew of the *Hispaniola* land on Robert Louis Stevenson's *Treasure Island* (1883), there is no mention of mosquitoes, but near the end of the tale Doctor Livesey is concerned to move away from the stockade up to the two-pointed hill. Ostensibly this is to keep guard on the treasure that Ben Gunn has disinterred, but also 'there to be clear of malaria'.

Seamen have long been wary of malaria, and with good cause. In 1585, Sir Francis Drake left Plymouth with 1,500 seamen and 800 soldiers in 29 ships. They went ashore for a short time in the Cape Verde Islands. Later, Drake wrote in his diary:

We were not many days at sea but there began among our
people such mortality, as in a few days there were dead
above two and three hundred men. And until some seven
or eight days after our coming from Santiago, there had
not died one man of sickness in all the fleet; the sickness
showed not his infection wherewith so many were stroken,
until we departed thence, and there seized our people
with extreme hot burning and continual agues.[17]

The typical incubation period for malaria is ten to twelve days,
but seven to eight is not uncommon. Drake lost a further 500
men when he reached the Caribbean, putting this down to
'first night air': 'who so is then abroad in the open air, shall
certainly be infected to death'.[18] It is easy to imagine mosquitoes
biting the newly landed sailors, celebrating their first landfall
in a more casual, carefree and perhaps inebriated manner than
they ought, paying less attention than they should to swatting
the bloodsuckers.

FIRST LINKS TO MOSQUITOES

Strangely, the link between mosquitoes and killer diseases was
first mooted centuries ago. There have been suggestions that the
Brahmin priest Susruta linked mosquitoes and malaria 2,500
years ago.[19] However, he made no precise judgement; he merely
differentiated between strongly venomous 'insects' like spiders
and scorpions (likening them to snake bites) and those with
mild poison like mosquitoes. More definite links are implied in
1572, when English writer Richard Hakluyt repeated details from
his correspondent Henry Hawks, who had spent five years in
Vera Cruz, Mexico:

This towne is inclined to many kinde of diseases, by reason of the great heat, and a certeine gnat or flie which they call a musquito, which biteth both men and women in their sleepe; and as soon as they are bitten, incontinently the flesh swelleth as though they had bene bitten with some venomous worme. And this musquito or gnat doth most follow such as are newly come into the countrey. Many there are that die of this annoyance.[20]

Into the nineteenth century, there continue to be many tantalizing instances of nearly, but not quite, making that correct link between malaria and mosquitoes. The great German explorer and writer Alexander von Humboldt made lengthy observations on mosquitoes during his journeys through Latin America in 1799–1804. His text is littered with remarks about their links to disease:

at the Orinoco, the banks of which are very insalubrious, the sick blame the mosquitoes for all their sufferings ... the insects irritate the epidermis, and stimulate its functions by the venom which they deposit in the wounds they make ... The frequency of gnats and mosquitoes characterises unhealthy climates only so far as the development and multiplication of these insects depend on the same causes that give rise to miasmata ... May not the mosquitoes themselves increase the insalubrity of the atmosphere?[21]

He ponders, since there are so many insects floating about in the air: 'we are led to inquire whether the presence of so many animal substances in the air must not occasion particular miasmata'.[22]

In what is perhaps his most portentous statement, Humboldt makes the direct suggestion that mosquito bites cause disease: 'wherever the air is very unhealthy, the sting of the mosquito augments the disposition of the organs to receive the impression of miasmata'.[23]

He finishes by suggesting that all will be well, health returned and the insects diminished, as soon as the rainforests can be cut down and the land cleared so that the rivers can be 'bordered with cottages, and the plains covered with pastures and harvests'. This had already started in the high cordilleras:

> From these fertile and temperate table-lands, from these islets scattered in the aerial ocean, knowledge and the blessings of social institutions will be spread over those vast forests extending along the foot of the Andes, now inhabited only by savage tribes whom the very wealth of nature has retained in indolence and barbarism.[24]

This sentiment, that the disease was withholding the advance of civilization, would be used again when the true nature of malaria was finally deciphered.

Just before the final pieces of the puzzle were dropped into place, the notion that biting flies might spread diseases was already very much 'in the air'. David Livingstone wrote about the tsetse fly in 1850:

> it is well known that the bite of this poisonous insect is certain death to the ox, horse, and dog . . . We lost forty-three fine oxen to its bite . . . symptoms seem to indicate what is probably the case, a poison in the blood, the germ of which enters when the proboscis is inserted . . . The poison germ, contained in a bulb at the root of the proboscis, seems capable, although very minute in quantity, of reproducing itself.[25]

It was later discovered that the bite of the tsetse fly spreads sleeping sickness.

At the same time, French physician Louis Daniel Beauperthuy, working in Venezuela, firmly identified the local mosquitoes, '*zancudo bobo*' (a species of *Aedes*), as being the carrier of yellow fever. He knew that 'the affection known as yellow fever, or black vomit . . . is in no way to be regarded as a contagious disease . . . The disease develops itself under conditions which favour the development of mosquitoes.' Although he incorrectly believed that the virus originated in the soil or water, he rightly believed that it was the mosquito bite, and the injection of infected saliva, that spread the disease to new victims: 'the mosquito plunges its proboscis into the skin . . . and introduces a poison akin to that of snake venom. It softens the red blood corpuscles, causes their rupture . . . and facilitates the mixing of the colouring matter with the serum'.[26]

In the early 1880s Albert Freeman Africanus King, a successful gynaecologist and obstetrician in Washington, DC, suggested that mosquitoes might spread malaria through their bites. At that time, he visited the US Department of Agriculture and spoke to the government entomologists Charles Valentine Riley and Leland Ossian Howard 'at some length'. 45 years later, Howard was to recall the meeting slightly apologetically: 'I am sorry to say that we gave him no encouragement. The idea appeared to us to be altogether too farfetched.'[27] King went on to publish his thoughts, but perhaps because he was in the wrong medical field, or he wrote in *Popular Science Monthly* rather than an academic journal, his suggestions were overlooked until examined in hindsight.

Today, malaria is the disease that everyone associates with mosquitoes, but malaria actually came third. Mosquitoes, it turns out, are responsible for a number of deadly and debilitating illnesses.

In 1877 Patrick Manson, medical officer with the Chinese imperial maritime customs, demonstrated by dissection under the microscope that one of the forms of filariasis (elephantiasis) was incubated in the bodies of mosquitoes. The disease, characterized by gross (elephantine) swelling of legs and scrotum, is caused by minute (0.2–0.3 mm / $\frac{1}{100}$ in long) parasitic blood worms accumulating in the lower limbs and blocking the lymphatic drainage vessels, resulting in fluid build-up, bloated flesh and thickening skin. Manson knew that an adult worm, 70–100 mm (3–4 in) long, could be found in the liver, and that the microfilariae, which blocked the blood vessels, were the larvae – but there was no intermediate form, and how did the worms move from one human to another? He settled on mosquitoes, because he knew that the blood worm had to move on to the next stage of its development in some agent 'capable of piercing the skin of the human body'. He allowed females of *Culex fatigans* to bite a filariasis sufferer, and made a series of dissections over several tense days. 'I shall not easily forget the first mosquito I dissected so charged. I tore off its abdomen, and by rolling a pen-holder from the free end of the abdomen to the severed end, I succeeded in expressing the blood the stomach contained.' Under the microscope: 'I was gratified to find that far from killing the filaria, the digestive juices of the mosquito seemed to have stimulated it to fresh activity.'[28] He went on to show that the worms taken in with the blood migrated into the body of the mosquito, grew and developed – first a digestive tract, then

An engraving from 1614 shows that filariasis (elephantiasis) was long known as a discrete disease. It was the first protozoan disease identified as being spread by mosquitoes.

genitalia. At the time, Manson (later Sir Patrick, Nobel Prize winner) thought that mosquitoes then died transferring these microscopic parasites into the water, and that humans developed the disease by drinking in infectious particles. Manson (and everyone else) was wrong; mosquitoes transfer the worms from person to person during their blood meals, but his initial discovery set the stage for great revelations ahead.

In 1881 Cuban doctor Carlos Finlay, overlooking the previous work of Beauperthuy, suggested yellow fever was spread by mosquitoes. This disease was intimately linked with the failure of the French effort to build a Panama Canal between 1882 and

SOLDAT ! PRENDS CHAQUE JOUR TA QUININE

Le Permissionnaire

Il a mal pris sa Quinine.   *Il a bien pris sa Quinine.*

Quinine was widely used as a febrifuge long before its specificity for malaria was discovered.

1889; 25 years earlier, the Panama railroad had exacted a horrible price, with 40 per cent mortality. Porto Bello on the Caribbean coast was described as 'an open grave ready to swallow all who resorted there'.[29] To dig the proposed canal, the French engineer Ferdinand de Lesseps was brought in after success on the Suez Canal. Much of Suez was cut through comparatively mosquito- and disease-free land; it was completed in 1869, after ten years of construction, and malaria only broke out seriously in 1877 when, by a convoluted irony, Italian workmen were blamed for bringing it. Central America proved different and with heavy disease loads from the start, the Panama project was eventually abandoned.[30]

It took nearly twenty years of back-and-forth mosquito research before, in 1900, American army surgeon Walter Reed finally proved that yellow fever transmission was by mosquito bite. It was, however, a success tinged with failure. At first, Reed did not believe Finlay's ideas and spent much wasteful time trying to prove some soil- or water-borne pathogen. Yellow fever is a virus, a speck of barely living material so small that, unlike filariasis, it cannot be seen with a light microscope and it passes through the ceramic filters that stop even bacteria. It also has a different modus operandi, and rather than simply multiplying in the body fluids, it disappears into the DNA machinery of the mosquito for up to a month before it returns to an infectious state. In September 1900, at the successful climax of the research, Reed's friend and assistant in Cuba, Jesse Lazear, died of yellow fever. Reed died in 1902, aged just 51, of a ruptured appendix. Two years later, armed with the knowledge to fight the mosquito, and the disease, the USA began a new assault on the Panama Isthmus, and although sickness continued to afflict the workers, the canal was completed by its better health-protected engineers and labourers in 1914, two years ahead of schedule. US government entomologist L. O. Howard later confirmed that, had he survived, Reed would undoubtedly have been awarded a Nobel Prize for his yellow fever work.[31]

The unravelling of malaria started in 1880, when French physician Charles Louis Alphonse Laveran, working in Algeria, found strange, moving particles in the blood of malaria sufferers. He deduced that these were a protozoan parasite. By 1884 he suspected that these parasites might also be found in the bodies of mosquitoes.[32]

The year 1897 was the pivotal year for malarial research. In that year, Ronald Ross, working in Secunderabad, in southeast India, found malaria granules in the stomachs of mosquitoes fed on a patient with the disease. Unfortunately, he was then posted to another part of India, but by Patrick Manson's intercession he was sent to Calcutta to continue his malarial research. Human malaria was not common in Calcutta, so Ross turned his attention to bird malaria and was able to trace the cycle of the parasite's development to a local mosquito species. But the mugwumps had not finished with Ross and he was now sent to Assam to study kala-azar (leishmaniasis, another protozoan parasite, this time spread by sandflies).

Meanwhile, still in 1897, with Ross chasing sandflies in Assam, Giovanni Battista Grassi, in Rome, proved that the female *Anopheles* mosquito was the human vector for malaria by successfully infecting a healthy man living in a non-malarial area by having an experimentally malaria-laden mosquito bite him. Medical ethics committees might baulk at this today, but it was the evidence that clinched the link between malaria and mosquito.

The final malarial breakthrough of 1897 came in dar es Salaam, in modern-day Tanzania, but then in German East Africa, where Prussian physician Robert Koch demonstrated that the chemical quinine destroyed the malarial parasites in human blood. Koch, especially, is credited with helping blow away the medieval humoral miasma idea of disease, and establishing the germ theory we now know to be correct. Earlier, in 1876, he had proved that anthrax was a bacterial infection and he had made similar discoveries with tuberculosis and cholera.

Quinine, as well as a remedy for fevers, was seen as a useful treatment of other disorders, including 'terrible itching'.

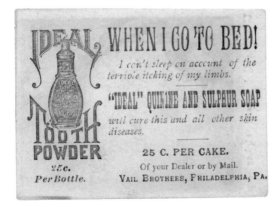

Use Ideal Quinine and Sulphur Soap

The exact details of who, when, how and why malaria was 'discovered' may be lost to the general public's psyche today, but it happened at a time of blossoming scientific enquiry, often labelled as the golden age of medico-veterinary entomology. The idea of a Victorian gentleman scientist labouring in some outpost of Empire, poring over his microscope, rattling Petri dishes and test tubes, and scratching endless letters to his contemporaries back in England, is a familiar image and one used regularly in literature, theatre and film. In *Holmes of the Raj* (2006), one of many modern sequel spin-offs from Sir Arthur Conan Doyle's popular hero, the famous London detective's sidekick, Dr John Watson, is portrayed as discovering the malaria–mosquito link, but in his usual gallant way he remains in the background and passes his observations to one Ronald Ross, medical Resident of Bangalore, and of course the rest is history.

Unfortunately, no such gentlemanly good sportsmanship really existed between the rival national scientific groups, and they all sought to claim as much of the discovery limelight as possible. In his later years, there was some unease when Ross took to 'much controversial writing'[33] as he vigorously fought the rival claims of the Italians. Writing in 1902, for example, Ross wrote to the same L. O. Howard who had not been very encouraging towards A.F.A. King's early malaria suggestions:

I think that the Italian school requires a little medicine in the shape of plain speaking. I suppose that you have seen the last effort of Grassi and Noe, who pretend that they have found out about *Filaria bancrofti* [the elephantiasis parasite]. As a matter of fact they have hardly ever seen one, much less found out anything about them. Believe me.[34]

When Howard visited the retired Ross in Putney Heath in 1927, the great man was no less vociferous. Despite having suffered a serious stroke that paralysed the left side of his body, Ross was as belligerent and inflammatory as ever:

> He showed us a big cabinet in which he had systematically filed and indexed all of the papers relating to his malaria work. He swore about the Italians, spoke of Grassi as a damned liar . . . He spoke of De Kruiff's book *The Microbe Hunters* [which he believed gave too much credit to Grassi] with profanity . . . He gave us each a copy of his latest paper on the Grassi claims . . . Grassi was a damned pirate.[35]

Despite Ross's and Grassi's rival competing claims, the understanding of malaria cannot be attributed to one single discovery. Ross continued to work on malaria for many years, often in difficult circumstances. Back in Secunderabad in 1907, he worked daily in the intolerable heat, without a punkah for fear of disturbing the delicate mosquito specimens he was dissecting under his worn and broken microscope, 'the screws being rusted with sweat from my hands and forehead, and my only remaining eye-piece being cracked . . . Fortunately my invaluable oil-immersion object glass remained good.'[36] He was rewarded by the further discovery of the next stages of the malaria parasite's life cycle within the body of the mosquito. In the end, Sir Ronald Ross, Nobel laureate, Knight Commander of the Order of the Bath, after whom roads, buildings, medical institutes, lectures and medals are named, received more than enough awards and accolades during and after his life, and he is certainly worthy to be nominated as the major determiner of malaria's cause.

Malarial transmission is not a simple case of infected blood being picked up from one person and arbitrarily transported to another by the passive dart of a mosquito's mouthparts. The entire complex life cycle of the parasite is intricately tied into the completely different physiologies of both human and mosquito hosts.

Malaria is caused by a tiny microbe called *Plasmodium*. An *Anopheles* mosquito infected with malaria injects anticoagulant saliva when it bites; it also injects spindle-shaped *Plasmodium* 'spore' cells, technically called sporozoites, which enter the victim's bloodstream. They end up in the liver, where they divide to produce new *Plasmodium* cells called merozoites. Some of these reinvade the liver while others pass into the bloodstream, where they enter the red blood cells. Inside these red corpuscles, they increase in size before again splitting into more merozoites. The red cells burst, ejecting haemoglobin (the 'mixing of the colouring matter with the serum' seen by Beauperthuy) and releasing the multiplied merozoites back into the blood to attack the liver again and yet more red blood cells. This repeating and *increasing* cycle of production within the red blood cells creates huge numbers of circulating merozoites and huge numbers of damaged red cells, often causing anaemia. When they rupture, the red cells also unleash toxins into the blood, and it is the cyclical release of these toxins, every two or three days, that produces the regularly recurring fevers for which malaria is well known.

While all this is going on, some merozoites take a different developmental pathway and form pre-sexual cells called gametocytes. These red cells do not rupture, but circulate in the blood waiting to be drunk down by another *Anopheles* mosquito.

Only when they are ingested into the mosquito gut do the gametocytes undergo further development and form the male and female cells (gametes), which combine to form fertilized cells called zygotes. The *Plasmodium* zygotes pass into the mosquito's intestinal wall, where they eventually develop into progenitor 'egg' cells called ovocysts, which divide and multiply to form large numbers of the sporozoites that started the whole process. The sporozoites migrate to the mosquito salivary glands and wait to be injected with the mosquito's next human bite. The parasite's development within the mosquito takes about fourteen days, and it was this hidden part of the cycle that had previously so confused the medical profession. It was too great a time lag to link individual malaria sufferers and threw any calculations about contagion times and transmission modes into complex disarray. It would, however, later prove to be an important fourteen-day window during which malaria outbreaks might be contained and controlled.

All the transforming cell types, from sporozoites to merozoites to gametocytes and zygotes, may seem ludicrously complex, but malaria's astonishing cycle of mosquito/human parasitism has a simple biological process at its heart – amplification. A small number of *Plasmodium* particles injected into a human victim reproduce vast numbers of themselves in the blood; all the better to be picked up by the next mosquito. A small number of these *Plasmodium* particles ingested by a mosquito again reproduce large numbers of themselves; all the better to be injected back into the next human victim to keep the cycle going. It works very well, and it has been working for at least eight million years when, according to one study, human malaria started to evolve away from the proto-malaria that infected our hominid ancestors.[37]

One of the most complicated things about malaria is that it is not one disease, but four (at the last count).[38] Four species of

Plasmodium infect humans (and plenty of others infect birds or mammals). Two of these, *P. malariae* and *P. ovale*, are rare; *P. ovale* is hardly known outside tropical West Africa. It is the 'big two' that have had the greatest effect on mankind. *Plasmodium vivax* is the most widespread, and the one reckoned to be behind ague in temperate climes. This is because it can develop in mosquitoes in much cooler regions ($15°C/59°F$ for at least one month; most of North America and much of Eurasia). The death toll from vivax is about 1–2 per cent of severe untreated infections during epidemics; higher than many other infectious diseases, but nothing compared to the last and most deadly malarial parasite. *Plasmodium falciparum* is the danger malaria of the tropics, and with a death rate of 25–50 per cent of severe untreated infections, is the disease that has been responsible for most of the malaria deaths in the world. This is a dark shadow of a disease that has probably killed more people on the planet than any other single cause, and which is still killing about one million people every year, mostly infants in sub-Saharan Africa.

Differences between at least three of the four parasites have been known, even if not fully appreciated, from time immemorial. They each have slightly different symptoms. The cyclical mass release of the blood-inhabiting merozoites, together with the fever-inducing toxins when the red blood cells burst, have a fairly fixed periodicity. With vivax, falciparum and ovale, there is a crippling sledgehammer attack of fever every 48 hours, traditionally called 'tertian' fevers, because they appeared every first and third day. Chaucer, in 'The Nun's Priest's Tale', warns not to 'get yourself with sudden humours hot; / For if you do, I dare well lay a groat / That you shall have the tertian fever's pain'. For *P. malariae* victims, the attacks come every 72 hours, so the term 'quartan' fevers is used, because they appeared every first and fourth day. In his *Inferno* (*c.* 1308–21), Dante speaks of 'one who

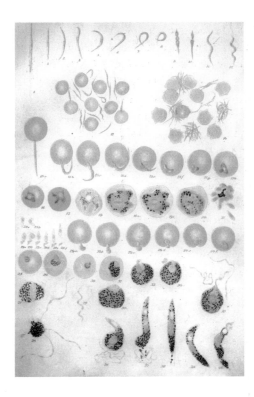

Fritz Schaudinn, blood cells being invaded by *Plasmodium vivax* parasites, 1903.

has the shivering of the quartan so near, / that he has his nails already pale, / and trembles all'.

Seasonality was also well known, especially away from the perennially warm tropics where the mosquitoes and disease were present all year round. On his travels through Arabia, noted traveller, linguist, soldier and spy Captain Sir Richard Burton relayed: 'In the summer, quotidian and tertian fevers (Hummah Salis) are not uncommon, and . . . are frequently fatal. The attack generally begins with the naffazah, or cold fit, and is followed by the al-hummah, the hot stage.'[39]

Physicians also noted the relatively low mortality rate of vivax, calling it 'benign tertian' fever, and the more deadly falciparum, which was 'malignant tertian'. Other differences are seen in the incubation period after being bitten by an infected mosquito – falciparum hit fast and deadly (as it did for Drake's crew) in 7–12 days, ovale after about 17 days, malariae 18–40 days and vivax (as suffered by Alfred Russel Wallace) anything from 15 days to a year. Vivax also had a dormant stage, which could remain, asymptomatic, in the liver for many months or years, only to recur spontaneously, without warning, after a long period of what seemed like cure. (Ovale, likewise, can have a 'resting' stage.) Differences between the various *Plasmodium* species also help to explain why it is that some people can survive inside the malaria zone, while others – usually newcomers – quickly fall victim to its fevers, febrile convulsions, delirium and, all too often, its rapid, fatal end.

When he received his Nobel Prize, on 12 December 1902, Ronald Ross stirringly summed up this effect on newcomers in his acceptance speech 'Researches on Malaria'. It's worth publishing part of it here, capturing as it does the imperial frustration that the disease engendered.

> Malarial fever is important, not only because of the misery which it inflicts upon mankind, but because of the serious opposition which it has always given to the march of civilization in the tropics. Unlike many diseases, it is essentially endemic, a local malady, and one which unfortunately haunts more especially the fertile well-watered, and luxuriant tracts – precisely those which are of the greatest value to man. There it strikes down not only the indigenous barbaric population, but with still greater certainty, the pioneers of civilization –

the planter, the trader, the missionary, and the soldier. It is therefore the principal and gigantic ally of Barbarism. No wild deserts, no savage races, no geographical difficulties have proved so inimical to civilization as this disease. We may also say that it has withheld an entire continent from humanity – the immense and fertile tracts of Africa. What we call the Dark Continent should be called the Malarious Continent; and for centuries the successive waves of civilization which have flooded and fertilised Europe and America have broken themselves in vain upon its deadly shores.

Powerful stuff. It was not unravelled until the last half of the twentieth century, but there is an underlying biological reason why Ross's European march of civilizing expansion (for which also read commercial exploitation) into Africa was much slower than in southern Asia and the Americas – resistance within the bodies of the indigenous population to attack from *Plasmodium* parasites.

It had long been known that newcomers, usually Europeans, were especially susceptible to malaria, and virtually every tropical African city has probably been described as a white man's grave at some point in its history. When researchers knew which microbes to look for in the blood, they often found that many of the indigenous population were infected, yet showed no disease signs. Knowing that they were surrounded by a walking reservoir of symptom-free carriers was justification for segregating the community – keeping the diseased natives away from the vulnerable expatriate colonists.

Today, two mechanisms of resistance are known. Across tropical Africa, 97 per cent of contemporary populations carry a gene in their DNA called 'Duffy antigen negativity', named after the haemophiliac in which the positive antigen was first found, in 1950. The antigen, on the surface of the red blood cell, is the door through which the malaria merozoites invade. The 'negative' gene – which means that the antigen is missing – is thought to have appeared, as a result of a random genetic mutation, 100,000 years ago. The negative gene does not disadvantage the carriers, but since the antigen is not there, *Plasmodium vivax* cannot invade the blood cells, and this prevents the disease from taking hold in the body. In effect, 97 per cent of the tropical African population – those carrying the Duffy negativity gene – are immune to vivax malaria.

Resistance to the more dangerous falciparum malaria is not so benign. Another series of random genetic mutations also took place in Africa (maybe also Arabia or southern India) 70,000–150,000 years ago, in the DNA that codes for haemoglobin (the oxygen-transporting red pigment in the blood cells). The mutation causes sickle-cell disease, so named because the altered haemoglobin changes the shape of the normally round red blood cells into long, thin sickles. The falciparum parasite cannot get into the sickle blood cells to multiply. Unfortunately, the sickle cells carry less oxygen, are shorter lived than normal red cells, and do not flow smoothly through the capillaries. These problems combine to create a parade of life-threatening complications from anaemia and kidney disease to stroke. An individual receiving a mutant sickle cell gene from one parent and a normal gene from the other, can also produce the normal haemoglobin, and normal round red cells. In this case, the sickle cells do not cause as great a problem, but do give some immunity to malaria. However, individuals receiving sickle cell genes from both parents have greatly reduced life expectancy, usually death before adulthood. In some West African communities, 25–30 per cent of the population carry a single copy of the sickle cell gene. This means around one in ten of the children born there will have the dangerous, ultimately fatal, double mutant gene combination. There is a very high price to be paid for falciparum immunity.

These discoveries, of blood parasites, mosquito vectors and partial immunities, start to make clear some of the historical conundrums about the origin of malaria and the spread of epidemics. Unlike smallpox, measles and the other dreadful contagious pandemic diseases, malaria needed two fuses to light the keg of disease gunpowder – an immigration of malaria-carrying humans, and the presence of suitable malaria vector mosquitoes.

Back in Tolkien's Midgewater Marshes, stout country hobbit Sam Gamgee is being eaten alive by midges and asks: 'What do they live on when they can't get a hobbit?' Little does he realize, he's just asked a very pertinent biological question. If humans (and maybe hobbits) are thin on the ground, mosquitoes will bite other animals, including wild birds and mammals and, in agricultural country, farming stock. For the relatively short-lived mosquito, this in effect dilutes the probability of malaria being passed on to other humans. If stock animals are bitten, they will not harbour the disease for long (or at all if their blood physiology is significantly different to that of humans), because they are almost inevitably slaughtered for their meat. Of course, eating, even raw, meat carries no risk of malaria infection. Biting of wild creatures can, very rarely, create a natural reservoir for the disease when no humans are about, but if mosquitoes evolve, say, bird-biting behaviour, they are unlikely to transfer their attacks back to humans; once learned, they stick to birds. In order for malaria to become the dreadful killer it is today, human population density had to achieve a critical mass. In Neolithic Africa, hunter-gather populations were just not dense enough to sustain the heavy malarial loads we see today. The disease was a 'minor' problem, allowing the immunities of Duffy negativity and sickle-cell anaemia to evolve.

In most of Europe, the chronically debilitating, but usually less deadly, vivax malaria was the cause of ague. Seasonal flooding affected the yearly patterns of mosquito abundance and human activities. Fenland drainage for agriculture started removing the mosquito breeding grounds long before any medical significance could be appreciated.

When Europeans arrived in the New World, they found sparsely scattered nomads in the north, and their Old World poxes devastated the metropolitan civilizations of the centre and south. Malaria was not a problem for many decades, perhaps even a couple of centuries, but increasing population in concentrated settlements eventually allowed the disease to run out of control. When the colonial powers decided on sugar cane economics around the Caribbean, the local indentured labour, mostly brought in from South America, succumbed quickly to the malaria which had become established in the relatively densely populated lowland settlements, so hardier, disease-resistant slaves, bringing their long-acquired immunities, were imported from Africa.

The fall of Rome, and the eclipse of the ancient Greek civilization, has recently been linked (through archaeological DNA studies) to the arrival of the much more deadly falciparum malaria into southern Europe around 450 CE. Until then, Europe had only to deal with the 'mild' vivax ague form of the disease.[40] High mortality, leading to economic collapse and civil chaos, is suggested by some to have resulted partly from the likely combined arrival of suitable falciparum vectors and falciparum carriers.

Was the arrival of rice, 2,500 years ago, with its mosquito-friendly aquatic cultivation, the spark that made malaria flare up in Japan? Increased trade, and the exchange of paddy engineering know-how, would also have brought infected individuals from China into the changing and increasing Japanese agricultural settlements.

The mysterious Mauritian malarial outbreak of 1866 is now explained with the crystal-clear vision of hindsight. Although malaria-infected immigrants arrived in a constant stream for two centuries, and their individual fits and tremors may have stayed with them all their lives, it was not until the accidental introduction (and subsequent breeding) of the key mosquito, *Anopheles gambiae*, from Africa, in 1866, that the disease could become established in the wider population. Until that year, there was no suitable mosquito vector on the island. Meanwhile, back on Stevenson's fictional *Treasure Island*, malaria should not have been a threat. Although it was in the malarial Caribbean, the secret island on Billy Bones's map was deserted, apart from Ben Gunn. He may have been a 'half-idiot maroon', but he was not ill with the fever. Even if malaria vector mosquitoes had been present, there would have been no pool of malaria-carrying humans to infect the newly landed adventurers.

At the end of the nineteenth century, the revelations of Manson, Ross, Grassi and all the other great medical men heralded the start of a new war against disease. The weapons were still in the making, but the enemy had been clearly identified. All across the world, mosquitoes were in the cross-hairs of the gun sights and the hunt was on.

6 The March of Progress

The discovery of links between mosquitoes and civilization-thwarting malaria transformed them, mutated them even, like B-movie monsters, into the objects of intense scientific study, and hastened an urgent search for eradication and 'cure'.

The searching was carried out both in the laboratory and in the tropical wilderness. There was a rush to establish centres of excellence for the study of the newly deciphered tropical diseases. In the autumn of 1898 (very shortly after that year of discovery, 1897), the two greatest port cities in Britain – Liverpool and London – became homes to such centres. Ronald Ross was the first senior lecturer, and later professor, at the Liverpool School of Tropical Medicine. Patrick Manson led The London School of Hygiene and Tropical Medicine, and a 'friendly rivalry' ensues to this day. Tropical medicine schools were also founded in Hamburg, Paris, Bordeaux and Harvard (Washington, DC). Their remit was to be both laboratory and expedition headquarters, as researchers were sent around the world to study endemic diseases and vectors, educate the local populace, train medical staff and bring back material for study and publication.

Many of these scientific academies had the word 'hygiene' in their titles. This was more than just a general nod to hand-washing and bodily cleanliness. It had more to do with sewage and stormwater run-off, which provided perfect mosquito breeding sites in seasonally flooded pools and poorly drained ditches. 'Mosquito brigades' dispatched from the various learned institutions would set about mosquito and medical surveys in any given target region, but most importantly they would find and destroy mosquito breeding habitats. Books of the time, such as *Mosquito or Man?* (1909) and *The Insect Legion* (1939), are full of edifying images showing pictures 'before', where rank pools and cluttered ditches were home to myriad wriggling larvae, and 'after', where neat, painted concrete gulleys and shining standpipes now allowed regular flushing through to prevent the flies from breeding.

The brigades were hailed as models of entomological, medical and organizational success. Malaria was quickly reduced in targeted towns and cities like Ismailia (near Suez), Port Said, Khartoum and Rio de Janeiro. The 'other' mosquito disease, yellow fever, was also targeted and, when a major epidemic struck New Orleans in July 1905, it was soon brought under control by the timely dispatch of tropical medicine practitioners.[1] This city outbreak was the perfect opportunity to try out a massive public information exercise. Mayoral letters were posted around town; free sulphur was offered for building fumigation; appeals were sent out to doctors for early disease notifications, and to the clergy to give mosquito- and yellow-fever-awareness sermons. Wednesday 9 August 1905 was a general clean-up day, designated for clearing discarded rubbish and so removing potential breeding sites, and the weekend of 2–3 September was chosen for general fumigation in order to kill as many mosquitoes as possible in one blow. Instructions were issued demonstrating how to seal and partition buildings using brown paper and glue to contain the fumigation gases. Isolation hospitals were created; their beds and rooms draped with acres of netting. An ordinance prescribed how water-storage tanks should be screened, with

A New Orleans yellow fever ward, netted off and ready to receive patients.

anyone failing to do so liable to a hefty fine of $25 or 30 days in prison. The concerted campaign was successful, and the city was free of the disease by the end of the month.

But not everything always went according to plan. In 1899, Ronald Ross was dispatched to Freetown in the British protectorate of Sierra Leone, tasked with reducing the awful malaria there. He and his brigade set about destroying the abundant mosquito breeding sites by spraying them with oil. Poorly funded at first, he did not have enough supplies or manpower, and he severely underestimated the size of the job. He redoubled his efforts and started a campaign to rid the city streets of bottles, tin cans, discarded tyres and all manner of rubbish where mosquitoes could breed in the rain slops. Despite his best efforts, the undertaking was a failure, and as soon as oil-spraying stopped, the mosquitoes were back in force. Today, the programme is remembered more for its impact on Freetown's litter.[2]

New Orleans
yellow fever poster.

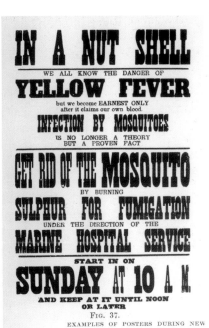

The mosquito-
proof hut used
during malaria
experiments near
Rome was so novel
that it warranted
its own picture in
Charles Aubrey
Ealand's *Insects
and Man* (1915).

It was not just staff from tropical medicine schools who were recruited to the cause of worldwide mosquito study. Colonial administrators, explorers and travellers roved the globe and, apart from their administrative (or military) day jobs, they were often encouraged to collect natural history objects – everything from pressed plants and animal skins to seashells and insect specimens. Stocking the museums of the world with disease vectors now became a high priority. The Natural History Museum, or British Museum (Natural History) as it was then, had long produced explanatory booklets on how to collect and preserve everything from fleas to whales and in 1904 E. E. Austen wrote their pamphlet, *Blood-sucking Flies, Ticks etc. and How to Collect Them*. It was regularly updated and revised through numerous editions for 22 years.

Mosquito-hunting success was mixed, though. Explorer and naturalist Robert Ernest Cheeseman collected many animals previously unknown to science during his journey across the Arabian Peninsula in 1923. He is credited with discovering Cheeseman's gerbil (*Gerbillus cheesemani*), but could not find any interesting mosquitoes, despite the locals' assertions that several of the oases had bad reputations for fever. He commented:

Mosquitoes were seldom heard, and their absence may almost have been considered a disappointment . . . I only found one species (*Culex fatigans*), one of the least harmful of the rapacious insects. These never once bit me, but they used to be heard passing over my head after the lamp was out. The lamp was hastily relighted in the hope that it would be an *Anopheles* at last.[3]

Slide-mounted mosquito. Scientific institutions across the world started to fill with specimens and images of potential vectors.

Sadly, it never was. Cheeseman may not have had much success, but elsewhere across the world entomologists collected huge quantities of material, from pinned mosquitoes and pickled larvae to dissected blood-and-gut samples on microscope slides. It was on the back of this upsurge in mosquito collecting that Frederick Vincent Theobald wrote his now classic four-volume, 2,459-page *Monograph of the Culicidae, or Mosquitoes*, published by the British Museum (Natural History) between 1901 and 1910. Theobald included around 600 species of mosquito known throughout the world at the time. There are now known to be more than 3,500 species. As it turned out, wherever entomologists swung a net, or just sat with their shirtsleeves rolled up, there were new mosquito species to find. In the Himalayas, larvae were found in mountain pools above 3,600 m/11,800 ft (quite contrary to the notion that mosquitoes are lowland flies); in the Far East, they occurred in rice paddies; they were also found breeding in mangrove swamps, in wells, in vehicle tracks, in

Henry Wellcome's
floating laboratory
near Khartoum;
it was towed
by the ss *Culex*,
visible on the
right.

hippopotamus hoofprints. This was not just an esoteric collection of new mosquito species that, once described and identified, were ready to be eradicated. Correct identification and understanding had real practical importance.

It very soon transpired that not all mosquitoes carry diseases. Malaria, for example, was only carried by *Anopheles* mosquitoes; about 100 of over 450 known *Anopheles* species *can* transmit the *Plasmodium* parasite, but only about 35 ever do so frequently enough to worry about. The most significant were *Anopheles funestus* and *An. gambiae* (which sparked the malaria epidemic in Mauritius). *Aedes aegypti* was the major yellow fever vector, *Culex fatigans* was the main filariasis species and *Ae. albopictus* was an important carrier of dengue fever. Since each mosquito species had evolved in a different place, in a different habitat, and often with different feeding habits or host preferences, it was sensible to try and catalogue mosquito diversity around the world. Understanding the enemy would be at the heart of winning the war against mosquitoes.

Recruiting the
'native collector'
was one way
of amassing
specimens.

Moving live mosquito specimens infected with malaria around the world required specialist equipment and stretched the ingenuity of entomologists.

FIG. 30. BOX DESIGNED BY DR. L. SAMBON FOR THE TRANSPORT OF MOSQUITOES

Back in 1930s Europe, for example, detailed taxonomic study showed that the ague/malaria vector, *Anopheles maculipennis*, was actually a mixture of several extremely closely related sister species. Two of these, microscopically identical as adults, but distinguished by their floating egg batches, occurred in the UK. One (form *messeae*) laid egg rafts crossed with dark bars, bred in inland pools, hardly ever bit humans and was not a disease carrier. The other (form *atroparvus*) laid egg floats with irregular markings, was widespread in coastal marshes, often came into buildings to roost and regularly bit humans. It was this latter form which had been mostly responsible for the historical spread of ague in lowland England.

Similar revelations were happening all across the globe as new species were found and described. One of the oddest – and, as it turns out, most ecologically interesting – of mosquito habitats is inside plants. In Britain, the potential malaria carrier *Anopheles plumbeus* regularly laid its eggs in flooded tree holes, where branches had broken off and left a deep gash allowing water to collect. But in the deep rainforests, another plant reservoir is used. The water-filled axils of bromeliads are used by several mosquitoes, including *Anopheles bellator*, a forest-dwelling malaria vector from South America. Growing on branches high up in the rainforest canopy, bromeliads are inaccessible to easy examination but occur in high densities where other potential breeding sites are few. New bromeliad-breeding mosquitoes are still being found and described today.

It is not just in the deep tropics that evolutionary divergence and the discovery of new forms and species is still going on. During the Blitz (1940–41), the beleaguered citizens of London escaped explosions in the bombproof deep tunnels of the Underground system, but were regularly bitten by mosquitoes; the common *Culex pipiens* had adapted to breeding in rainwater puddles along the subterranean railway lines. Although indistinguishable under the microscope from its surface-dwelling relatives, it showed significant differences in behaviour, and was designated as a separate species, *C. molestus*.[4] It bit mammals (the mice and rats infesting the tunnels, and the daily herds of human commuters and shelterers) rather than birds; it bred all year round in the mild, temperature-stable atmosphere rather than just in summer; and it could, if necessary, lay its first batch of eggs without a blood meal (a regression, perhaps, to the evolutionarily primitive autogenous physiology of species with larvae that develop in especially nutrient-rich water). Recent DNA studies show that *C. molestus* is, indeed, distinct from the above-ground *C. pipiens*, and they will not interbreed, an odd evolutionary situation that should really have taken 100,000 years rather than the 100 or so that the tunnels have been in existence. Furthermore, each of several populations on different London Underground lines were also genetically distinct; in another 100 years time there may be separate Circle Line,

Metropolitan Line and Jubilee Line mosquito species in the tunnels below London.[5]

Insect specimens last hundreds of years, but the greatest legacy these dead mosquitoes leave will not be their corpses pinned in museum drawers, but the truly enormous scientific literature spawned about them. Virtually every country in the world has

Adult and larval mosquitoes identified by their body positions.

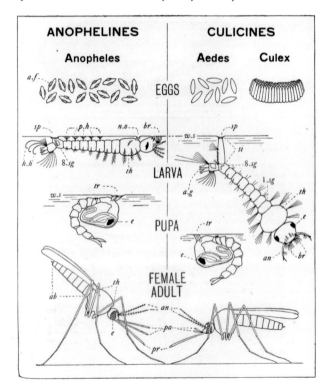

Every part of mosquito anatomy is subjected to intense scrutiny in 20th-century monographs.

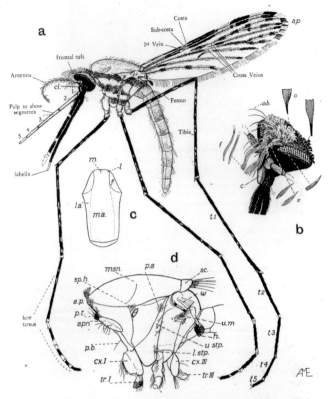

Fig. 87. Diagrams showing the nomenclature of parts in adult *Anopheles*. **a.** Whole insect (*A. gambiae*, female) in side view, showing the main parts of the body; one palp raised and denuded of scales to show segments (1-5); *t1-t5*, the five segments of the hind tarsus; *ap.*, wing apex; *cl.*, clypeus. **b.** Head seen obliquely to show scaling; individual scales from the occiput (*o.*), vertex (*v.*), and frontal tuft (*f.*) enlarged to show average shape; *c.*, clypeus; *o.b.*, orbital bristles. **c.** Upper surface of thorax (mesonotum): *m.a.*, median area; *l.a.*, lateral area; *f.*, fossa; *m.*, median and *l.*, lateral position on anterior region of mesonotum where scales are commonly attached. **d.** Side of thorax, showing areas, bristles, etc.; *a.p.*, apex of thorax; *apn.*, anterior pronotal lobe; *cx.I*, front coxa; *cx.III*, hind coxa; *h.*, haltere; *l.stp.*, lower sternopleural or mesepisternal bristles; *msn.*, dorsum (mesonotum or scutum); *p.a.*, prealar tuft of bristles; *p.b.*, propleural bristle; *p.t.*, pronotal scale tuft; *sc.*, scutellum; *sp.h.*, spiracular hairs or bristles; *tr.I*, front trochanter; *tr.III*, hind trochanter; *u.stp.*, upper sternopleural or mesepisternal bristles; *u.m.*, upper mesepimeral bristles; *w.*, base of wing.

(From Evans)

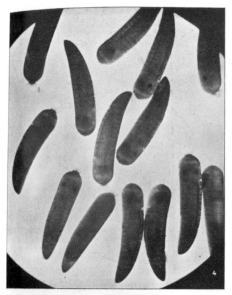

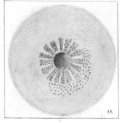

Fig 11. — Appendice em forma de taça colocado do polo rombo de um ovo de *Culex fatigans*, visto de cima, com forte augmento. Mostra uma granulação orientada em sentido radial, originando-se ahi uma figura semelhante á do sol.

Fig. 4. — Grupo de ovos de *Culex fatigans*, vistos com augmento mais forte. Já estão bastante adiantados no seu desenvolvimento. No polo rombo percebe-se, em alguns, distinctamente um appendice em fórma de taça, apparelho de funcção problematica.

Fig. 6. — Parte de uma jangada fresca de ovos de *Culex fatigans*, vista perpendicularmente de cima; aspecto microscopico com fraco augmento. A jangada acha-se sobre uma lamina de vidro, naturalmente sem laminula de cobrir. Os circulos escuros são os ovos; os espaços claros são os interstícios. Notabilissima é a regularidade geometrica da arrumação dos ovos.

Fig. 10. — Aspecto de mesma granulação da fig. 9, vista na peripheria, com o tubo do microscopio abaixado; fortissimo augmento.

Fig. 5. — Dois ovos do mesmo grupo, photographados com augmento bastante forte; posição lateral. O ponto escuro, pelo lado anterior, indica o olho da larva; o estreitamento atraz do primeiro quinto o limite entre o thorax e o abdomen, sendo d'este ultimo bem visivel a segmentação.

Fig. 12. — Joven larva de *Culex fatigans*, de um dia de idade, vista com regular augmento, immediatamente depois de morta. Note-se o siphão respiratorio anal bastante comprido e as antennas compridas.

Fig. 18. — Desenho da parte terminal do corpo da mesma larva, em escala menor que na fig. 17. No segmento anal vêem-se ao lado dos 4 folliolos branchiaes sómente ainda 4 cerdas compridas e vistosas, mas não o tufo ulterior.

Fig. 16. — Larva bem crescida, quasi adulta, de *Culex fatigans*; augmento fraco. Antennas mais compridas do que as escovas rotatorias do apparelho bucal; siphão respiratorio comprido; folliolos branchiaes do systema tracheal de dimensões antes reduzidas.

Fig. 13. — Larva da mesma idade, que a da fig. 12, morta já ha alguns tempo e tratada com solução de fuchsina para tingil-a, processo que todavia não deu o resultado desejado, chegando-se a vir mais da estructura interna na observação da larva viva.

Fig. 21. — Desenho da parte aboral da mesma larva da fig. 20, em escala menos ampla. Note-se o apparecimento de um respeitavel tufo anal de cerdas.

Fig. 15. — Duas larvas da mesma idade que as da fig. 14, e nas mesmas circumstancias, porém alimentadas com carmim para salientar melhor o tracto intestinal. Observe-se o comprimento relativamente grande do siphão respiratorio.

Fig. 26. — Pupa (chrysalida) de *Culex fatigans*, vista lateral; augmento fraco. Note-se a forma e o comprimento do piston respiratorio no thorax.

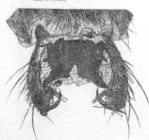

Fig. 28. — Aspecto geral do apparelho genital exterior do macho de *Culex fatigans*, (♂) sito na parte posterior do corpo, photographado com fraco augmento.

Fig. 24. — Desenho, feito com a camara lucida, de algumas escamas isoladas do „pecten", do 8º segmento, (8ᵉ) visto com augmento microscopico bastante forte.

Fig. 23. — Antenna de uma larva adulta de *Culex fatigans*; vista photographica com augmento bastante forte.

college or university or hospital departments of tropical medicine (and hygiene) dedicated to the study of insect vectors and their parasite burdens. There are also countless national and international bodies, military institutes, the World Health Organization, health and disease relief charities and multinational pharmaceutical companies. From these institutions there is an endless stream of scientific journals dedicated to studying mosquitoes and the diseases they spread.

The first wave of mosquito-centred writing, following the disease revelations of the 1890s, was a basic show-and-tell analysis of how the flies could be told apart, where they lived and developed, and what their disease links might be. For example, in January 1901 the newly founded *Journal of Hygiene* carried two special mosquito articles in its first issue. The first paper (40 pages of it) gave an extensive list of *Anopheles* sightings in Britain, and compared this with recorded cases of ague.[6] The accompanying map, showing the individual mosquito localities, is one of the first such distribution maps ever to be published. An expanded, poster-sized map, produced with military precision, and a work of art in itself, was published as a follow-up in 1918.[7] The second *Journal of Hygiene* article is a standard text on *Anopheles* biology and structure. It is encyclopaedic in its descriptions of the insects and is illustrated by some exquisitely delicate engravings of adult flies and early stages.[8]

There then followed a veritable blizzard of books, pamphlets and scientific papers on medical entomology, tropical medicine and mosquitoes in particular. Many of these are the nuts and bolts of everyday science – lists of new mosquito species, identification keys, technical descriptions and diagrams, observations on life histories and biting habits, dispersal strategies and mating behaviour. On the whole, the science of these early books and papers has been superseded, but they still have curiosity value

previous:
Every stage of the mosquito life cycle was studied and documented in minute detail.

today. What comes across most is that this was a time of great human endeavour, and the struggle against mosquitoes and disease was seen as a test of European colonial mettle. Books with rousing titles like *Mosquito or Man? The Conquest of the Tropical World* (1909), *The Insect Menace* (1931) and *The Insect Legion* (1939) are filled with an enthusiasm bordering on triumphalism. The rhetoric is truly monumental. On the one hand, there was an acceptance that malaria still had a disease stranglehold on the tropical world:

> India is like Prometheus bound by chains of apathy to the rock of expediency and financial stringency, while the vulture of malaria devours the vitals of her people.[9]

But now that tropical diseases were understood, it would only be a matter of time before they would be conquered:

> malaria, yellow fever, plague, Malta fever, sleeping sickness and tropical anaemia. In these diseases it is now only a question of efficient administration and organisation in order to bring about their total abolition. The result is a triumph of the advancement of medical knowledge, and it is not too much to say that the twentieth century will be known in the annals of medicine by the immense progress which medical science has made into the causes and prevention of tropical diseases, discoveries which show clearly the role of insect life in the transmission of disease, and, in consequence, the most effective way of stopping disease . . . The narrative would appear more like a fairy tale were it not based upon easily accessible reports and figures.[10]

The dour message put forward by Ross in his Nobel acceptance speech, about the barbarism inflicted by malaria on the Developing World, was now to be countered:

> not only has the study of tropical diseases conferred an increased benefit upon the science of medicine, it has given new and undreamt-of advantages to commerce, to civilisation, and to administration in tropical countries. To-day we receive regular reports from all parts of the tropical world showing what is being accomplished – the new areas and territories wrested from decay and handed over to civilisation . . . Thus a situation which at one time appeared hopeless is now, on the contrary, full of hope, and the tropics are rapidly becoming possible for Europeans.[11]

The tone of the times is seemingly imperious and arrogant when tropical colonies and possessions are being discussed in terms of their commerce and exploitation rather than of the lifting of human suffering. This was, however, the genuine voice of the early twentieth century – sometimes patronizing, but always forthright and confident. It was not reserved solely for the empire; this attitude resonated through domestic studies, too.

One of the more entertaining is the delightful dissertation by Alfred Moore Hogarth, *British Mosquitoes and How to Eliminate Them*, published in 1928. Moore Hogarth was founder and chairman of the 'College of Pestology (Inc.)'. His aims were to identify and discuss UK mosquito species and to comment on their nuisance and elimination. He frequently makes mention of how his institute is part of these great works.

Malaria does not really come into Moore Hogarth's equations. There is a palpable note of regret: 'Apart from a few outbreaks, notably at Sandwich and in the Isle of Sheppey, this danger has, or, at any rate, appears to have, disappeared.'[12] (He's recalling outbreaks in army rehabilitation camps during the First World War.) Instead, he has to emphasize the nuisance factor of the flies, and in a chapter ominously entitled 'The Gravity of the Menace' he lists the twenty or so British deaths between 1919 and 1925 from septicaemia after mosquito bites became infected. Sad and devastating though these individual deaths inevitably were, they pale into insignificance beside the millions of malaria victims worldwide.

He has to bolster his warnings by further listing cases 'of severe illness directly or indirectly due to mosquito bites'. To do this, he does what publicity-seekers still do today – he reports on some celebrities. We soon learn that 'in 1924, Sir Gerald du Maurier was bitten in the face while spending a brief holiday at the seaside. He had to undergo a slight operation and was absent from the stage for a fortnight.' That same year, 'a mosquito bite incapacitated Lady Terrington, MP, from attendance at the House of Commons for some time', and 'last summer, that distinguished cricketer, Mr G. O. Allen, was bitten by a mosquito while playing for Middlesex against Notts at Lords, and was unable to take any further part in the match'. British mosquitoes might not be spreading malaria, but they could still be a tad irritating.[13]

It was not long before mosquitoes and malaria started to appear in popular literature, too. The writings of Joseph Conrad, tragic analyses of empire, are permeated with disease, as the 'white man' (often blue-eyed) suffers or witnesses illness, fever and death in the brooding tropics. 'The Lagoon' (1896) is set around a hut perched on piles in a backwater creek somewhere in the Malay Archipelago; inside, a woman is dying of high fever and Conrad's scene-setting conjures up the perfect

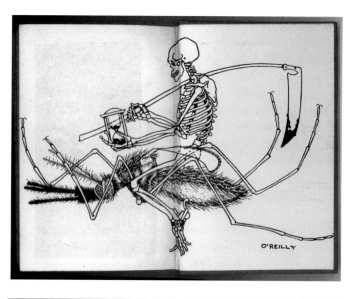

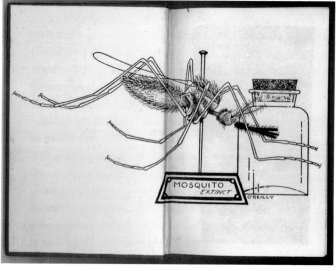

malarial swamp. In *Heart of Darkness* (1899), men 'were dying of fever at a rate of three a day'. Conrad contracted malaria on the four-month steamboat voyage in the Congo while he was researching this book. As the medical discoveries in the real world unfolded around him, Conrad, whether knowingly or not, takes them into his narratives. *The Rescue* was begun in 1896, but was not completed until 1919, by which time mosquito and malaria research was at fever pitch. Early chapters show little interest in insects, but in later sections his characters are plagued by them.[14]

In the popular children's book *Little House on the Prairie*, by Laura Ingalls Wilder (1935), chapter Fifteen is called 'Fever 'n' Ague'. The whole family fall ill with fevers and chills, and receive help through the kindness of strangers. The book is written in the form of reminiscences from Wilder's childhood in nineteenth-century Kansas, before mosquito links were made.

The delightful endpapers by O'Reilly from Alfred Moore Hogarth's essay on the dangers of British mosquitoes, 1928.

By the early 20th century the malaria mosquito was well enough known to be offered on collectable trade cards; this one from the series 'Toxic and disease-spreading arthropods of Congo' was from Oxo, which 'tastes fine and restores strength'.

GIFTIGE OF ZIEKTEVERSPREIDENDE GELEEDPOTIGEN VAN KONGO
5. De Mug van de Malaria : Anopheles gambiae (Giles)
Oxo Bouillon : smaakt fijn en herstelt de krachten

$8\frac{1}{2}mm.$

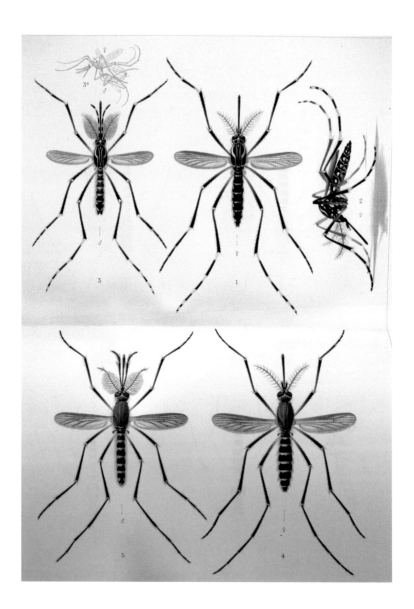

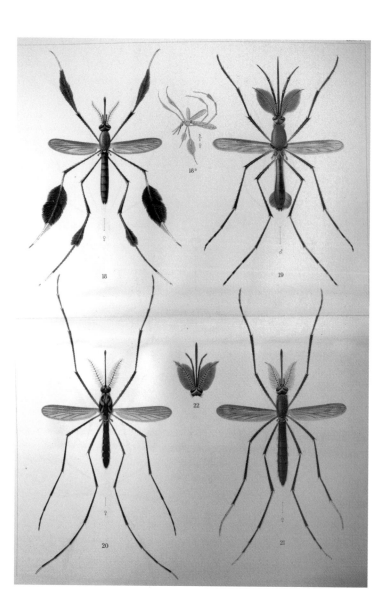

18ª

18   19   20   22   21

previous:
Mosquitoes from
around the world
came in startling
shapes and
colours.

Some tales are not so uplifting. In H. P. Lovecraft's 'Winged Death' (1933), the narrator of the story is an invertebrate biologist famed for his work in Mombasa on the insect transmission of 'remittent fever', but now undermined by the whisperings of a jealous colleague. Accused of scientific plagiarism and thwarted in his aim of a knighthood, he seeks revenge on his accuser, whom he intends to kill using a strange new disease-carrying insect, the devil-fly. The bloodsucking fly is not a mosquito, but Lovecraft's descriptions of persistence and tenacity sit well for any such attacker. His final, superbly gothic, twist is that the mysterious blue-winged insect, instead of injecting fatal disease parasites, drains its victim of more than blood – it removes the soul.

The rapid and enthusiastic growth in mosquito study during the early and mid-twentieth century continued to bring knowledge and insight, real advances in conquering malaria and the other insect-borne diseases, and a greatly improved awareness in the general public. Handbooks for medical practitioners and textbooks for students began to fill with text and diagrams of mosquitoes and malaria. The mosquito monographs of the time are authoritative and clear (if slightly repetitive), and they excel in the beautiful quality of their illustrations – mosquitoes could still be wondered at in their delicate forms and strange patterns. Some of these images are still in use today. The coloured plates by A. J. Engel Terzi, first used in 1906 for a monograph entitled *Illustrations of British Blood-sucking Flies*, were reused for an updated edition in 1939, then again for a popular mosquito identification guide in 1990.[15] They are as good today as any modern pictures of the flies.

Academic entomologists continued their enthusiasm for finding and documenting new mosquitoes, but what was really needed was a practical way of controlling or killing them.

可怕的瘧蚊.帶着死魔到人間来散佈瘧疾.

要防瘧　先滅蚊

malaria

Everywhere, the mosquito had become the spectre of death.

Spraying the breeding sites with motor oil was all very well, but it could contaminate water drunk by animals and humans. Luckily, humans had been battling other insect pests for centuries, and the search for a malaria cure moved away from mosquito hunting to the promising uses of potions and poisons.

7 The Theatre of War

The nineteenth century was a period of great change in the entomological world. Insects went from being the objects of desire (to be marvelled at in glass-topped cases) to objects of derision, to be destroyed. The naturalists were changing too; a growing band of 'economic' entomologists turned to studying agricultural pest species, and they were already well versed in the techniques of control and eradication.

Around mid-century, naturalists began to realize the sheer enormity of insect numbers and diversity, and this gave the study of insects a profound zoological gravitas. In 1855 the Entomological Society of London, 22 years old, was granted a royal charter by Queen Victoria, a prelude to it later becoming the *Royal* Entomological Society at its centenary. The list of early fellows reads like a who's who of biological study at the time, and includes some of the most influential natural scientists of the day. They include: Charles Darwin and Alfred Russel Wallace (propounders of evolution by natural selection), Henry Walter Bates (traveller in the Amazon region after whom Batesian mimicry is named), Frederick William Hope (founder of the Hope Department of Entomology at Oxford University), John Lubbock (First Baron Avebury, natural scientist, banker, archaeologist and the MP who gave us bank holidays) and Edward Newman (founder and editor of *The Zoologist* and *The Entomologist*).

These mainly wealthy gentlemen were usually concerned with finding and describing new species; brightly coloured beetles and butterflies were popular, but there was not much work on mosquitoes. They proposed new classifications and elucidated life histories. They were doing what we might today call the basic science, science for its own sake, or perhaps for the wonder of it all. But emerging around them was a study of insect pests that attack crop fields and stored food. Soon to be added to this list of pest species were the vectors of disease – very notably mosquitoes.

The 'economic entomologist' was led by agriculture with its increasing mechanization and a desire for improved yields. As if to rub in the fact that this new breed of entomologist was very different, the doyenne among them was a woman – Eleanor Anne Ormerod. Very much part of the landed gentry of the time, her autobiography makes charming and fascinating reading.[1] In 1877 she published a short pamphlet on 'injurious insects', which she distributed to 'interested persons'. The whole thing snowballed and she began a 24-year stint of producing and publishing – at her own expense – large annual reports, from her tangled web of correspondents. She went on to receive a wide range of accolades, including medals and honorary fellowships from scientific organizations around the world. When the insect/disease intrigue started to unravel at the end of the nineteenth century, it was natural that economic entomologists such as Ormerod would become involved with mosquitoes. Ormerod's message, typical of the time, was clear: insects eat our crops and threaten us with starvation; the answer was to poison the lot. Among the heavy-handed treatments meted out were suggestions such as sprinkling them with soot, drenching them with petroleum emulsion or tar spray, hosing them down, knocking them down, hand-picking them, and

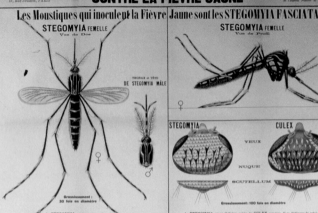
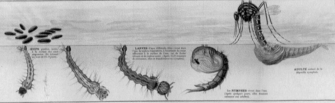

squishing them. These worked well enough, but sometimes a more ferocious tactic was required.

The 'mosquito menace' (its status now upgraded from a mere nuisance to disease-spreading plague) came on the crest of another serious insect battle. During the 1860s and '70s, the undaunted eastward spread across the USA of the Colorado beetle, *Leptinotarsa decimlineata*, a major pest of potatoes, had fuelled economic entomology and its spin-off in chemical insecticides. When the Colorado beetle was accidentally introduced into Europe, near Mülheim in Germany in 1877, it was seen as an international emergency. The area was cordoned off by troops, doused with kerosene and the entire 5-ha (12-acre) plot was torched.

WEAPONS OF MASS PROTECTION

Fire was an effective, if blunt, instrument, but it was the use of targeted pesticides that loaded the armoury in mankind's favour. By far the most widespread insecticide of the day was Paris green, a strongly coloured pigment used in paints. The quite likely apocryphal tale goes that in the 1860s a US farmer painted his windows bright green and threw the unused dregs over potatoes infested with Colorado beetles. The beetles dropped dead. Paris green was a copper acetoarsenite, usually mixed with lead arsenate, and it was pretty deadly to anything (including people). It did not take long to discover that Paris green was also highly effective at poisoning mosquitoes and their larvae.

Unlike the moneyed scientific gentlemen (it was almost exclusively a male preserve) of a generation before, the new entomologists were keen to give their expertise and advice a professional air.[2] Much as physicians were able to make a diagnosis and then write out a prescription for medicines, the

Yellow fever awareness posters identify *Stegomyia* as the vector, and urge water butts be screened.

The hand-held insecticide spray revolutionized tropical farming.

PLATE I

WAR ON THE MOSQUITO IN THE PANAMA CANAL ZONE. APPLICATION OF LARVICIDE FROM A KNAPSACK SPRAYER

(See p. 114)

entomologists were now able to offer their own prescription against insect pests – Paris green. Ormerod, who had by now set herself up as unofficial national entomologist, wrote several books on garden and agricultural pests as well as her annual reports, and by 1892 she had composed her own epitaph: 'She introduced Paris green into England.'[3]

Where chemicals
are not enough –
the scorched earth
policy.

PLATE V

BURNING UNDERGROWTH IN WHICH MOSQUITOS TAKE SHELTER,
PANAMA CANAL ZONE

(See p. 114)

Paris green and other chemical poisons were seen as very modern alternatives to the rather old-fashioned soot and sulphur dusting. It was with substances like Paris green in mind that hand-pumped sprayers were developed (the 'Fountain', 'Eclipse' and 'Number 1 éclair' were typical inspiring brand names). Various other poisons enjoyed liberal application, including sprayed fuel oil, oil-soaked sawdust and kerosene (via the patented 'Kerowater' pump). 'Panama mixture', named after the canal it helped to build, was a mixture of 680 l (180 US gal./ 150 imp. gal.) crude carbolic acid, 90 kg (200 lb) rosin (from naphtha distillation of pine stumps) and 15 kg (30 lb) caustic soda, all diluted in five times its volume of water or mixed with crude oil. Any of these ingredients would have been enough to kill the embattled mosquito larvae, but Paris green was the application of choice and by the 1920s it was being dusted by the ton from tractor-driven machines, and later sprayed across entire swamps by aeroplane.

Despite the attraction of an easy spray to kill mosquitoes and their larvae, the assault on malaria was really three-pronged. As well as killing the adult flies (and now their larvae), the anti-mosquito offensive was based on preventing bites by the use of bed nets and the almost miraculous medical properties of

Pouring kerosene into swamps was the usual anti-mosquito measure, seen here in a comic postcard from 1908.

quinine, a drug extracted from tree bark. This rather grandly termed 'integrated control methodology', is still at the heart of many anti-malaria campaigns.

Mosquito nets now came to mean not just night-time solace (as celebrated by Alfred Russel Wallace); they kept the disease vector from poisoning the blood. There had been a time when bed nets were seen as effeminate; it suddenly became foolhardy not to use them. To make them even more effective, they (and

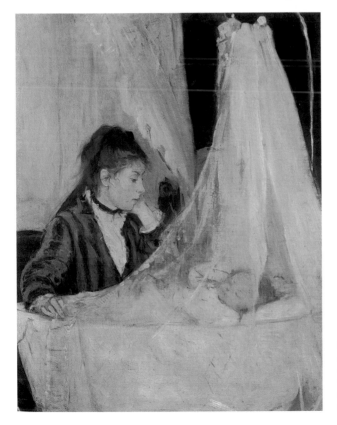

Mosquito nets come in all shapes and sizes. Berthe Morisot, *Le Berceau* (The Cradle), 1872, oil on canvas.

clothing) were doused with anti-mosquito concoctions with names like 'Black-fly Dope' and 'Sketo-nox', as well as strong-scented repellents like citronella oil or obvious poisons like carbolic acid.

Bed nets became part of every traveller's essential luggage. They came in every conceivable size and shape, for hats, beds, dinner tables, hammocks. Today, no military encampment or tropical hotel bedroom would be complete without the ghostly drapery, but it took some education to get here. In *Tintin in the Congo* (1931), Hergé's hero sleeps peacefully under his bed net. Optimistically, he bids Snowy the dog goodnight: 'Luckily, everyone knows that mosquitoes don't bite dogs.' Nobody told the mosquitoes, though, and Snowy spends a fitful night, eventually finding shelter under a coat. In the morning, Tintin offers some sympathy: 'Oh! My poor Snowy! You're bitten all over.

The benefits of a mosquito net are manifold: no painful bites and bumps, good looks and the loving adoration of the girl.

DORS TOUJOURS SOUS TA MOUSTIQUAIRE

Au réveil

S.S. d'ÉTAT du Service de SANTÉ. M.P.A.O. N°17

Il n'avait pas de Moustiquaire.   *Il a bien dormi sous sa Moustiquaire.*

John Singer Sargent's *Mosquito Nets, Valdemosa, Majorca*, 1908, shows Sargent's older sister Emily and her friend Eliza Wedgwood reading books under protective nets. The Sargents called the net a *garde-manger*, a protection from eaters rather than disease-spreaders, although malaria was a possibility in Majorca.

That's what happens when you sleep without a mosquito net.' Sage words. The book, the second of Hergé's Tintin series, is still regarded as controversial, with its stereotyped and racist portrayal of Africans. According to Hergé's biographers, the author was much influenced by his publisher at the time, and was instructed to show Belgian youth more about the value of colonialism.[4] Leaving aside Tintin's patronizing and sometimes despising attitude to the Congolese, he certainly gets across the message about mosquito nets.

The third line of defence against malaria came from the mysterious property of a neotropical jungle tree. Before modern Europeans made ready contact with the First Nations of the Americas, in 1492, the bark of the dogwood tree, *Cornus florida*, was boiled up to produce a painkilling and sleep-inducing draught.[5] When malaria first started to spread across the New World, it was natural that this traditional medicine was used.

Indeed, it appeared to give some relief against the symptoms of fever and pain. Other traditional tree barks (poplar) and roots (sarsaparilla) produce chemicals not unlike aspirin (originally derived from willow bark in Europe). The true breakthrough came in the sixteenth century, when the Spanish 'discovered' a real fever-breaking tree bark on the east slopes of the Andes.

The embroidered and, as it turns out, wholly invented tale of popular legend has it that the Countess of Chinchon, wife of the Spanish viceroy to Peru, was cured of her tertian fever by an elixir of powdered cinchona bark, which she then gave to the citizens of Lima and then to Spain. Unfortunately, historical research shows that the viceroy's first wife died in Spain before he ever left for Peru, and his second wife lived a very healthy life.[6] The origins of cinchona use may be lost in myth, but the brew that came out of the bark was a miracle.[7] It banished malaria. As Koch was later to show, in that cusp year 1897, the active ingredients killed the malaria parasites in the blood.

News of this marvellous medicine slowly permeated the world. During the 1640s, supplies of ground bark were making their way from mission stations in the Andes, back to Rome. There was some scepticism about 'Jesuit powder' from the Protestant nations, but it was in London in the 1650s and throughout most of Europe by the 1670s. Harvest and transport was labour-intensive and arduous, and it remained very expensive, but trade expanded. Control of cinchona was a great power, and in the early days the Spanish sought to maintain a royal monopoly. Contraband supplies were often blighted by 'bad bark', or the powder was cut with other substances. For 250 years, international trade conflicts, wars and poor understanding of drug actions hampered the general availability of antimalarials. Cinchona trees were planted around the world to supply the different European powers, but success varied. The British attempts in southern India were plagued with transportation losses, and the trees that were finally planted produced only low-grade bark. It was the Dutch plantations in Indonesia that transformed the market, and by the early twentieth century, Java was producing 90 per cent of the world's quinine.[8]

Gradually, the price of quinine came down, but across the tropics, it was usually the wealthier expatriates who used it. In India, the bitter quinine was mixed with alcohol to make it more palatable, giving rise to the British taste for 'Indian tonic water' mixed with gin. Despite early advertising claims, by the time branded tonic water was industrially brewed, the quinine content was so low it would have had negligible antimalarial effect.

During the Second World War, supplies of quinine were disrupted. In January 1942, when the Japanese invaded Java, they effectively took control of the world's antimalarials. This proved a real incentive for chemical companies to come up with a synthetic alternative. Biggles, the British airman personified,

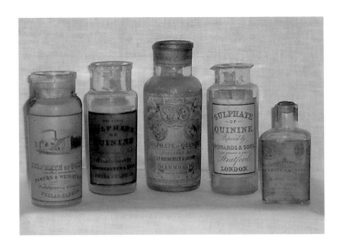

An assortment of Victorian quinine bottles.

suffered bouts of malaria in *Biggles in Borneo* (1943); when the attack came on without warning in mid-flight, he shouts 'Can't see', and his younger sidekick, Ginger, has to grab the control column. Later, travelling through northern India in *Biggles Goes Home* (1960), it's Ginger's turn to have 'the fever'. He is given a dose of Atebrin, a proprietary name for mepacrine (quinacrine in the USA), one of the first synthetic quinine substitutes to become widely available.

THE PROPAGANDA MACHINE

As the whole globe descended into the chaos of the Second World War, malaria was an extra enemy on almost every front. Apart from the obvious dangers of sending men to fight in the jungle, the mass movement of armies in and out of malarial zones was set to play havoc with international health policies. In 1941, when the USA entered the war, malaria was in full retreat from North America. The USA could not afford to have its domestic population under the shadow of a disease threat from returning soldiers, or the general hardships of a wartime economy. But the USA was ready and the next step was obvious – a Disney film.

In 1943, the wartime US government commissioned the Disney studios to make *The Winged Scourge*. Although only ten minutes long, it combines clear information with typical Disney wit, and delivers its life-saving message with power and dignity. Beginning with a wanted poster, 'Public Enemy Number 1 . . . wanted for wilful spreading of disease and theft of working hours', the voice-over describes the 'sickness and misery to untold millions' spread by this 'tiny criminal . . . what will she find to steal here? Only a little blood, which this man, wracked with the chills and fever of malaria, will never miss.' The jittery

In Disney's short film *The Winged Scourge* (1943), a once pretty and profitable farm falls into decline because the farmer failed to follow a few simple mosquito controls.

music emphasizes the mosquito whine and impending doom as the 'bloodthirsty vampire', now infected with the parasite, descends to the bare arm of the successful farmer, peacefully smoking his pipe on the veranda of his well-tended home. At the time, malaria was still present in parts of the USA, and although it was the milder vivax form, as the film correctly describes, 'this man will not die, but neither will he truly be alive, for he will be continually in poor health . . . will lose all he has worked for'. A huge mosquito assuming the proportions of a monster now towers over the house, which lies in ruin and neglect.

This is a grim message, but now comes the theatrical twist, and with a lightening of tone, the solution is offered. 'Are there six or seven people in the audience who will volunteer to help us combat this evil?' Up pop the Seven Dwarfs. Standing to attention and saluting to a bugle fanfare, they immediately set to work to protect their thatched cottage in the woods from the mosquitoes and their dread malaria. Sneezy and Doc cut water weeds to let the fish get at the wigglers; Happy sprays oil on the surface to kill the wigglers; Sleepy and Grumpy drain pools full of them; and, with the help of a trio of songbirds, Bashful dusts the swamp with a hearty draught of Paris green. Meanwhile, indoors, Dopey is dishing out a green spray from his éclair-style handpump against adult mosquitoes hiding in the chimney. Sealing cracks in the floors, covering the doors and windows with screens and putting nets over the beds allows the dwarfs to 'live in health, safety and happiness'.

In that same year, 1943, at the start of increased US fighting in the dangerous falciparum tropics of Southeast Asia, the cartoon talents of another famous American institution were called upon to promote the message to the troops – Dr Seuss. In the 1960s, Theodor Seuss Geisel achieved success with cats in hats, star-bellied sneetches and a grinch, but during the 1930s he

Copr. 1936 Stanco Inc. (Adv.)

"Quick, Henry! The Flit!"

In the 1930s, Theodor Seuss Geisel (Dr Seuss) drew cartoon adverts for Flit insect spray; his barb-nosed mosquitoes were later to be used for a national malaria awareness campaign.

drew advertising pictures and satirical cartoons. He had had notable success with the Flit insecticide campaign ('Quick, Henry, the Flit' was a nationally known catchphrase), so it was natural that he was chosen to illustrate a mosquito awareness campaign for the US military.[9] 'This is Ann . . . she drinks blood. Her full name is Anopheles mosquito and she's dying to meet you.' The GIS are warned: 'Ann moves around at night (a real party gal) and she's got a thirst.' To keep themselves fit and healthy, they are urged to take care of their bed nets, use repellent, avoid evening skinny-dipping and keep away from the 'lousy native villages'. The message is clear: 'a guy out cold from malaria is just as stiff as the one who stopped a hunk of steel . . . she can make you just as dead as a shell can'.

Seuss's distinctive, barb-nosed Anopheles Ann later appeared in one of the Private Snafu cartoon shorts, *It's Murder She Said . . .* (1945). An acronym of 'situation normal, all fucked up',

Snafu the dolt GI was created by the US Army Air Force Motion Picture Unit during the Second World War, and the cartoons, produced by Warner Brothers, were a vehicle for various public information messages. The irresponsible Snafu was the butt of endless calamities, suffered because he did not follow simple advice. Under attack from anti-mosquito operations and now past her best, Ann's been having a hard time lately, what with sprays, nets and swamp-clearing. Nevertheless, she was able to bite Snafu, who refused repellent, left his bed net in tatters and walked around with his shirt off. Ann passes round the snap-shots of her conquest to her friends: 'A smart operator can still sneak in for a one-night stand.'

Seuss used the nose again for one of several cartoons to promote US defence bonds and stamps. Armed with a spray

'This is Ann, she's dying to meet you.' Dr Seuss's Anopheles Ann was central to the US War Department's malaria awareness campaign.

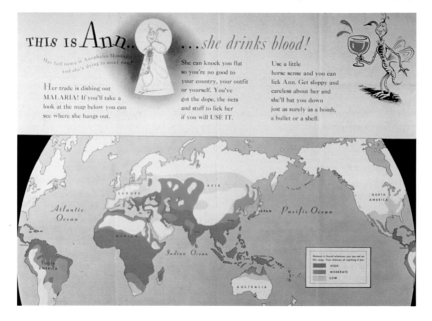

THIS IS Ann.. ...she drinks blood!

Her full name is Anopheles Mosquito and she's dying to meet you!

Her trade is dishing out MALARIA! If you'll take a look at the map below you can see where she hangs out.

She can knock you flat so you're no good to your country, your outfit or yourself. You've got the dope, the nets and stuff to lick her if you will USE IT.

Use a little horse sense and you can lick Ann. Get sloppy and careless about her and she'll bat you down just as surely as a bomb, a bullet or a shell.

ENEMIES BOTH!

IT'S YOUR JOB TO HELP ELIMINATE THEM

☆ U. S. GOVERNMENT PRINTING OFFICE : 1944—O-601850   NAVMED 141-D

MALARIA

The USA was focused on two enemies during the 1940s: Emperor Hirohito and the malaria mosquitoes in the battle-grounds of the Pacific

can so labelled, a stars-and-stripes-top-hatted American eagle prepares to exterminate swooping, beaked mosquito versions of Hitler and Hirohito (and a small, fat Mussolini). What must have been much to the delight of Seuss's colleagues back at the pesticide company, the advert also proclaims 'Quick, Henry, the Flit'.

In an era before television, public information poster campaigns were renowned for their style and power. They were works of art. Two mosquitoes in hats and gloves take tea, while

DON'T GO TO BED WITH
A MALARIA MOSQUITO
★ SLEEP UNDER A NET! ★ KEEP IT
REPAIRED! ★ TUCK IT IN! ★
*BE SURE NO MOSQUITO IS INSIDE
WAITING FOR YOU*
FIGHT THE PERIL BEHIND THE LINES

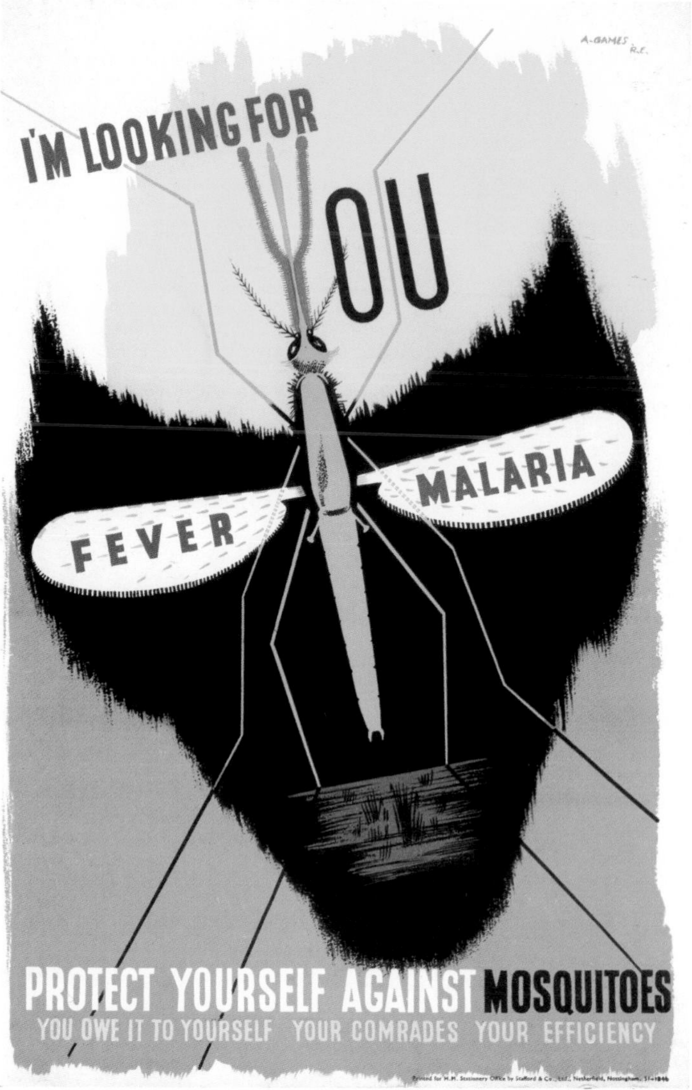
A. GAMES R.E.
I'M LOOKING FOR YOU
MALARIA
FEVER
PROTECT YOURSELF AGAINST MOSQUITOES
YOU OWE IT TO YOURSELF YOUR COMRADES YOUR EFFICIENCY
Printed for H.M. Stationery Office by Stafford & Co., Ltd., Netherfield, Nottingham.

The message may have moved on from simply health information to clothes marketing, but the clever poster just can't be beat.

previous:
The malaria mosquito did not respect battle fronts, so soldiers are urged to 'fight the peril behind the lines'.

A masterpiece of dramatic poster art.

one offers 'But my dear! You *must* try the troops.' The tea is the giveaway – this one was aimed at British Commonwealth troops. Some of the most effective images are also the simplest messages. The boldly stylized mosquito graphic, wings labelled 'fever' and 'malaria', against a dark, skull-shaped shadow, states baldly: 'I'm looking for you.' Another shows Uncle Sam gripping in one hand a bespectacled, swastika-wearing Hirohito, and in the other a mosquito labelled 'malaria'; the unequivocal slogan is 'Enemies both! It's your job to help eliminate them.' These joint enemies are again linked in a US Navy poster from 1945 stating: 'Man-made malaria, 6 in 10 mosquitoes breed in water in unnecessary ruts, abandoned roads, blocked ditches, fox and shell holes.' It shows the mosquito with stereotyped facial features and the rising sun of the Japanese imperial military flag on its wings. Although these images may smack of jingoism today, they were a necessary part of the propaganda of the day in the 1940s. This was war, and it was against both humans and mosquitoes.

Modern symbols from the art of the road sign and black-and-yellow hazard stripes, but the message is the same: don't be bit.

Not wishing to belittle modern poster artists, the genre is still well stocked with striking and elegantly graphic images. 'Fight the Bite' invites us to 'join the swat team against West Nile virus'. And we just know that the boxer stands no chance in the spoof event poster offering: 'You vs the malaria-infected mosquito.' I'm still not sure, though, about the strange, mixed metaphor given by the Utah Tobacco Prevention and Control Program, which shows a mosquito with the wrong number of legs, the wrong number of wings and the slogan 'Don't let the mucky mouth mosquito bite you.'

Ironically, tobacco smoke, particularly from pipes and cigars, was once regarded as a good mosquito deterrent, and was perhaps slightly easier on the nose than Wallace's brazier of burning cow dung. Not only were pipe- and cigar-smokers supposedly more immune from attack, but by some undisclosed metabolic serendipity, they were claimed not to suffer so severely if bitten. Nicotine was also once a widely used insecticide. It was hardly ever used against mosquito larvae because its toxicity is lost on them, and anyway, other much more potent chemicals soon became available.

A Chinese poster from 1970 offers anti-mosquito and anti-malarial advice.

Paris green, in the 1860s, was just the start. Paints continued to be a good source of new poisons, with London purple (a calcium arsenite) and white arsenic (trioxide of arsenic) proving useful. Terpenes were powerful-smelling hydrocarbons extracted from pine wood-oils. Anabasine (also found in paints) was similar to nicotine and could be extracted from tree tobacco. Pyrethrum was a powerful natural insecticide made from the dried flowers of several daisy-like flowers. The trouble with many of these naturally occurring chemicals was that the original source needed to be laboriously harvested, then the active ingredients had to be concentrated and distilled, without destroying their toxicity. And, many natural derivatives do not persist very long in the open environment; they are soon denatured and toxicity is lost. Spraying pyrethrum in an apple orchard against codling moth in June was fine; even if the pyrethrum broke down quickly, it had still done its job on that single application and all of the highly seasonal moths had been destroyed. Spraying a house, or a factory or a school against mosquitoes was useless if the poison decayed and was unable to kill mosquitoes arriving the next week.

The end of the nineteenth century was also a time when chemists began to better understand the nature of substances in terms of their atoms and molecular structures. In the early twentieth century, they started to think of ways to build their own chemicals to mimic or better those they found in nature. Thiocyanate became one of the first synthetic insecticides to be manufactured on a commercial scale, in 1929. There has been a constant stream ever since. The most important, most widely used and the best known was a neatly symmetrical double phenyl organochloride first synthesized by student pharmacist

Othmar Zeidler in Austria in 1874. However, it remained a laboratory curiosity until its insecticide ability was noted by Paul Müller in Switzerland in 1939. For the next 30 years, DDT, short for dichlorodiphenyltrichlorethane, became the single most important insecticide in the world.

DDT is a colourless, almost odourless, crystalline substance that is hardly soluble in water, but highly dissolvable in organic solvents and oils. Unlike naturally occurring biological compounds, which vary in concentration from source to source, and season to season, DDT could be manufactured to exact specifications. It did not rely on the erratic import of a natural product. It also lasted for weeks or months on walls and ceilings where mosquitoes rested. And, since it was a contact insecticide, entering the mosquito's system through the feet when they landed, this residual toxicity gave it a staying power not matched by natural products.

During the Second World War, DDT was a secret weapon for the Allies, allowing them to spray living quarters and swamps against malarial mosquitoes (and each other against typhus-spreading lice). After the end of the war, it was a newsworthy item for the national press that DDT was to be released to the general public, because it had been taken off the army's 'scarce' list. DDT was launched onto the public psyche, wholeheartedly, with fanfare and celebration. It went under scores (maybe hundreds) of brand name aliases marketed by a network of chemical companies. They went to town in naming it, to capture the eye of the householder and the landowner. There was the obvious and bland (Cotton Dust, Tree-mist, Dawson #4 Insecticide, Mothene, New Larvex); the perky (End-o-pest, Pest-b-gon); the punning (Pestroy, Knoxout); the blunt (Jap Beetle Killer, Killer Dust); the science-fiction futuristic (Zerdane, Anofax, Gyron, Aavero); and the just plain odd (Panda, Top, Dairy mist, Dampo).

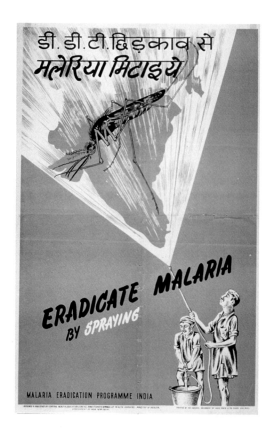

डी. डी. टी. छिड़काव से
मलेरिया मिटाइये

ERADICATE MALARIA
BY SPRAYING

MALARIA ERADICATION PROGRAMME INDIA

In this Indian anti-malarial poster from the 1950s little attention is paid to protective clothing.

Dr Seuss would have been pleased that DDT found its way into Flit Fly and Mosquito Killer. My own favourite is Kybosh.

Whatever the name on the can, the active ingredient, DDT, was the major selling point, as knowledge of its insect-toxicity spread. A wonderful advert appeared in *Life* magazine, showing a housewife, cow, dog, rooster, apple and potato all singing 'DDT is good for me-e-e.' The Sherwin-Williams Research Laboratories, makers of Pestroy, put out a film short, *Doomsday for Pests*

(1946), partly animated with newspaper-reading and newsreel-watching bugs running for their lives from this new mass-killing terror of cockroaches, ants, and, of course, mosquitoes. As well as promoting Pestroy's own brand, the film is full of praise for the efficacy, toxicity and (to humans and pets) safety of its prime ingredient – DDT.

Although DDT was first manufactured and used against insect disease vectors, it soon found other niches in agriculture, gardening and around the home. Production went up. At its height, in 1970, 175,000 tonnes were produced. DDT worked well. It was cheap. The sheer volumes of domestic spray cans on the shelves of gardening stores and supermarkets spoke volumes. So, too, did the easy availability to financially stretched developing countries. It was effective. Without doubt, it was the most effective control for mosquitoes anywhere – DDT use during the third quarter of the twentieth century was estimated by the World Health Organization to have saved over 25 million lives. And it was safe. Its effect on insects was as a nerve poison, causing the neurones to fire spontaneously, inducing spasms and eventually death. To mammals, and especially to humans, it showed very low toxicity; their nerves worked differently. Paul Müller was awarded the Nobel Prize in Physiology or Medicine in 1948.

> A mosquito was heard to complain
> That a chemist had poisoned his brain.
> The cause of his sorrow
> Was para-dichloro-
> Diphenyltrichloroethane.[10]

8 Environmental Chaos

DDT was the wonder chemical of the twentieth century. Wherever it was used, there were astounding results. In January 1946, Italian malariologist Alberto Missiroli astonished his audience at the Istituto Superiore di Sanità (Department of Health) when he proposed to stop all the previous measures to counter malaria – spraying breeding sites with larvicide, use of screens and bed nets, quinine prophylaxis and land reclamation. Instead, he suggested, they should just spray DDT in buildings. In 1949 and 1950, for the first time in over 2,000 years, there was not a single death from malaria in Italy, Sicily or Sardinia.[1]

Unfortunately, not everything was going as well as the manufacturers might have wished. There were some concerns about DDT's toxicity to fish, and there were anecdotal reports of domestic cat illness and deaths. The commercial importance of DDT made the quiet worries and complaints easy for the powerful manufacturers to ignore, and things went ignored for a long time; but in the end, all it took was a letter from an old friend.

In January 1958 Olga Owens Huckins wrote to her friend Rachel Carson, enclosing a copy of a letter she had just written to the *Boston Herald*, complaining of bird deaths after local DDT spraying against mosquitoes. Carson, a former biologist with the US Bureau of Fisheries, and by now a successful science

The great expectations held for DDT have been realized. During 1946, exhaustive scientific tests have shown that, when properly used, DDT kills a host of destructive insect pests, and is a benefactor of all humanity.

Pennsalt produces DDT and its products in all standard forms and is now one of the country's largest producers of this amazing insecticide. Today, everyone can enjoy added comfort, health and safety through the insect-killing powers of Pennsalt DDT products . . . and DDT is only one of Pennsalt's many chemical products which benefit industry, farm and home.

GOOD FOR FRUITS — Bigger apples, juicier fruits that are free from unsightly worms . . . all benefits resulting from DDT dusts and sprays.

GOOD FOR STEERS — Beef grows meatier nowadays . . . for it's a scientific fact that — compared to untreated cattle — beef steers gain up to 50 pounds extra when protected from horn flies and many other pests with DDT insecticides.

Knox Out FOR THE HOME — helps to make healthier, more comfortable homes . . . protects your family from dangerous insect pests. Use Knox-Out DDT Powders and Sprays as directed . . . then watch the bugs "bite the dust"!

Knox Out FOR DAIRIES — Up to 20% more milk . . . more butter . . . more cheese . . . tests prove greater milk production when dairy cows are protected from the annoyance of many insects with DDT insecticides like Knox-Out Stock and Barn Spray.

KILLING SALT

CHEMICALS

97 Years' Service to Industry • Farm • Home

GOOD FOR ROW CROPS — 25 more barrels of potatoes per acre . . . actual DDT tests have shown crop increases like this! DDT dusts and sprays help truck farmers pass these gains along to you.

Knox Out FOR INDUSTRY — Food processing plants, laundries, dry cleaning plants, hotels . . . dozens of industries gain effective bug control, more pleasant work conditions with Pennsalt DDT products.

writer, took up this report, and started to delve into similar events. In 1962 she published *Silent Spring*. The book opens with a Lovecraftian evocation of sinister change in an idyllic rural landscape. She begins:

> a checkerboard of prosperous farms, with fields of grain and hillsides of orchards . . . foxes barked in the hills and deer silently crossed the fields . . . along the roads, laurel, viburnum and alder, great ferns and wildflowers delighted the traveler's eye . . . The countryside was, in fact, famous for the abundance and variety of its bird life.

But:

> Then a strange blight crept over the area . . . mysterious maladies swept over the flocks of chickens; the cattle and sheep sickened and died. Everywhere was the shadow of death. The farmers spoke of much illness among their families . . . There was a strange stillness. The birds, for example – where had they gone? It was a spring without voices . . . only silence lay over the fields and woods and marsh.[2]

Carson's opening chapter is eerily similar to H. P. Lovecraft's short story, 'The Colour Out of Space' (1927). In a similar New England backwater, the story's narrator discovers a plot of land strangely devoid of life. The plants and animals become grey and brittle, and exhibit a slight phosphorescence. The farmer and his family are struck by illness and insanity. In this case, the cause of this otherworldly blight is a meteorite that had crashed into the well. We never quite discover what alien chemical (or being, perhaps) is in the well, but the rising sense of dread, as

During the 1940s the insecticide DDT was actively promoted as being good and healthy.

the poison spreads and clues emerge, has eerie parallels to Carson's unfolding investigation.

The underlying fugue of Carson's groundbreaking book was the devastating effect of indiscriminate use of highly toxic poisons across the environment. DDT was a name on everyone's lips. Insecticides were sprayed with such cavalier abandon that whole neighbourhoods were poisoned, and it was non-target organisms that suffered. Chemicals were washed away in the water run-off and entered the rivers, killing fish and polluting drinking water. In 1959, pellets of Aldrin (an organochloride similar to DDT) were scattered so thickly against Japanese beetle in the Detroit suburbs that the ground was blanketed like snow. This killed the beetles, a notorious invasive alien pest, but also their predators and parasites. The toxin was absorbed by earthworms, and by the birds that ate them. The very chemical property that gave the synthetics their value – their long biological life – meant they were not broken down by the birds' metabolism; instead they were accumulated in the body fat, a substance biochemically very similar to the liquid oils in which DDT was sprayed. DDT caused shell-thinning in birds' eggs, which were quite literally crushed underfoot in the nests.[3] It was the demise of the birds that triggered Huckins to write, and it was the silence of the birds departed that gave Carson's book its title and chilling message.

The appearance of *Silent Spring* is widely regarded as the signal event that started the modern environmental movement.[4] It was serialized in the *New Yorker*, and soon made its way into the *New York Times* bestseller list. The book and its accusations were discussed by national governments, the international media and the general public. Those chemical pesticides, once lauded as scientific miracles, were now damned as environmental pollutants. DDT was banned in Hungary in 1968, Sweden in 1970, Germany and the USA in 1972 and, eventually, in Britain in 1984.

Back in the 1950s and '60s, environmental poisoning was only one of the rising biological issues sparked by indiscriminate DDT use. Mosquito resistance to DDT had started to appear as early as 1956.[5] Likened to evolution in action, inconsistent DDT use meant that some mosquitoes, with chance mutations in the DNA responsible for the nerves it normally poisoned, were immune (or at least resistant) to the chemical. They survived and passed on this mutated gene to their offspring. Soon hardier generations had replaced the susceptible insects and new, resistant populations were no longer affected by DDT. Perhaps not surprisingly, the first species to show this resistance was one of the key malaria vectors in Africa, *Anopheles gambiae*, and one of the first fears was that insecticide spraying would cease to have any control over the disease in the area.

At this same time, vague, dystopian, science-fiction notions of radioactivity, genetic mutation and alien invaders were mixed into an anxiety of general biological upheaval. Hollywood, ever keen, but not the best measure of scientific understanding, now launched a series of outlandish giant insect horror movies. This was the time of *Them!* (1954), often cited as the worst film ever made, in which giant mutated ants the size of automobiles maraud through New Mexico. In *The Deadly Mantis* (1957), a volcano dislodges a 60-m (200-ft) praying mantis locked in Arctic ice for millions of years. In *Monster from Green Hell* (also 1957), wasps sent into space in a test rocket return and crash-land in Africa, where they transmogrify into green giants.

Everything got mixed up in these now dated vignettes. Despite the importance of mosquitoes, we had to wait until 1993 for *Skeeter* and 1995 for *Mosquito*. Both feature giant, mutated bloodsuckers, the first arising from dumped toxic waste, the other from feeding on decaying aliens killed in a flying saucer crash. Although 40 years too late, the films do not disappoint in their clichéd, B-movie horror styles, with rampaging giant insects, explosions and a lot of people screaming.

The word 'overkill' comes to mind now when we think about the tons of toxic chemical strewn over the landscape to kill mosquitoes. When the Monty Python team set about their *Mosquito Hunt* (1970), it was overkill that made the whole sketch funny. As they mock entomologists, game hunters and Australians ('I love animals, that's why I like to kill 'em'), they set off to stalk the insect with bazooka, machine guns and high explosives. The ground smokes as they finish the insect off ('There's nothing more dangerous than a wounded mosquito'), but the bombs and bullets they dispatch are relatively harmless compared to the almost unimaginable volume of chemical insecticides used in the real world.

It is funny, now, because we have forgotten the burden of ague and the nightly irritation of persistent biting attack. Malaria went from the USA by the 1950s and the National Malaria Society was officially disbanded in 1952. The last recorded case in Britain was about the same time. In the space of 25 years, one generation, killing mosquitoes went from being an unpleasant necessity to a joke. Another generation on, and memories of mosquito dangers are lost still further; we become ever more urbanized, and windows stay shut as houses benefit from double glazing, central heating and air-conditioning.

The earth-shaking discoveries of the 1890s, and the epiphany of understanding when the mosquito–disease knot was unravelled, fell upon a society ripe for the knowledge. It all coincided with similar discoveries about the spread of microbes by houseflies, and revolutions in sewage disposal and piped water delivery. But the novelty has faded. To some extent, those great

Mosquito was a 1950s-style horror B-movie, made in the 1990s. The giant mosquitoes were anatomically correct on screen, but the video cover is pleasingly daft, showing an insect with the wrong number of wings.

MOSQUITO

"...PURE TERROR..."
—CINEFANTASTIQUE

"...FROM THE CROWN
PRINCE OF HORROR..."
-FANGORIA

**MILLIONS OF YEARS OF EVOLUTION
HAVE JUST BECOME MANKIND'S WORST NIGHTMARE.**

ACME FILMS, LTD. And EXCALIBUR MOTION PICTURES In Association With ANTIBES, INC. Present a GARY JONES Film MOSQUITO Starring GUNNAR HANSEN
RON ASHETON STEVE DIXON RACHEL LOISELLE TIM LOVELACE Executive Producer ANDRE BLAY Executive Producers LARRY MAGID MARC SHULMAN
ALAN KAPLAN Music By ALLEN LYNCH RANDALL LYNCH Visual Effects Supervisor RICHARD JAKE JACOBSON Edited By TOM LUDWIG BILL SHAFFER
Production Designer JEFF GINYARD Lighting Director GEORGE LIEBER Director of Photography TOM CHANEY Original Story By GARY JONES
Screenplay By STEVE HOOGE TOM CHANEY GARY JONES Producer DAVID THIRY Producer ERIC PASCARELLI Directed By GARY JONES

R RESTRICTED
UNDER 17 REQUIRES ACCOMPANYING
PARENT OR ADULT GUARDIAN
© 1994 Skeeters Limited Partnership

HEMDALE
HOME VIDEO, INC.

mosquito discoveries were only the beginning; research contin-ues today. New diseases and new vectors are being found, but details become ever more focused and refined, and the minutiae of mosquito life become ever more abstruse. The current wave of mosquito research is erudite in the extreme, but the papers published in arcane journals are usually well beyond the scope of the general reader or educated layman. DNA analysis of indi-vidual mosquito genes, scanning electron micrographs of obscure body parts, molecular analyses of blood-digesting enzymes, iso-topic labelling of physiological pathways and genome mapping of *Plasmodium falciparum* all add to the corpus of accruing facts, but with an increasingly technical scientific jargon and complex mathematics, they are outside the understanding of the general public and are generally ignored by the press.

This has led to the strange situation that, although scientists learn more and more about mosquitoes and their diseases, the general public (including the policy- and decision-makers of government) learns less and less. General 'knowledge' of how and why mosquitoes spread disease is being watered down and replaced by caricature and myth. For many people, mosquito knowledge is slowly becoming a mosquito stereotype. This is not helped by the increasing emergence of the mosquito brand.

9 The Mosquito Brand

Mosquitoes bite (sometimes in common parlance they sting) and this has made them useful when it comes to naming things that would benefit from a painful association. This is not something new; the mosquito brand is very old.

Mosquito was a popular name for warships (as was *Gnat*). The earliest I can find was a privateer brig (possibly spelled *Musqetto*) fitted out for the Virginia State Navy and launched from Portsmouth, Virginia, in 1777, during the American War of Independence.[1]

HMS *Musquito*, a Royal Navy cruiser brig launched from Great Yarmouth in 1804, spent the Napoleonic Wars in the North Sea and Baltic, escorting transports. Then for several years she sailed off St Helena, 'guarding Napoleon', but taking time off to capture the occasional slave vessel. This was maritime biting at its best.

Meanwhile, President Jefferson, downsizing the US navy, commissioned a series of small gunships, in the hope that manoeuvrability and speed would outweigh puny size. They were deemed pathetically useless in the 1812 Anglo-American war, and became known, rather disparagingly, as the 'mosquito fleet'. But a similar mosquito fleet is credited with routing buccaneers from the Florida Keys around the same time. The term was used more endearingly for the large fleet of privately owned ferries

Although nothing is written in the white text box, the sentiment is clear: bloodsucker. This light-hearted poison-pen postcard was addressed in 1905 to Mr Charles Frazer, Assistant Tax Collector in Springfield, Massachusetts.

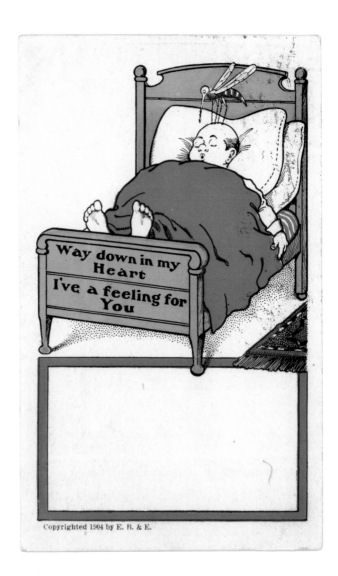

Way down in my Heart I've a feeling for You

Copyrighted 1904 by E. B. & E.

JUL 24 1912 ┊ 13275099 ┊ NO TITLE-PAGE & INDEX ISSUED

Double-Page Color Portrait of Woodrow Wilson in this Issue.

PUCK BUILDING, New York, July 24th, 1912.

VOL. LXXII. No. 1847. ┊ PRICE TEN CENTS.

Puck

TO SWAT 'EM IS WASTE OF TIME.
Pour Oil, and Plenty of It, on the Thing that Breeds Them.

Always irritation personified, the mosquitoes on the cover of this issue of *Puck* magazine from 1912 represent corporations benefiting from high protective tariffs.

and other boats plying the Puget Sound in Washington State in the early twentieth century.

There have been several other HMS *Mosquito*es, including an Aerial class gunboat launched from Pembroke in 1871, a torpedo boat destroyer launched in 1910, and a gunboat sunk during the

So far the provenance of this mosquito plate has defeated analysis. Could it be from the officer's mess aboard one of the many HMS *Mosquito*es?

Dunkirk evacuation in June 1940. During the Second World War, the Royal Navy had a shore establishment of the same name at Alexandria, in Egypt. In keeping with naval tradition, the 'stone frigate' bore the name as if it were a ship. The irony of the name was probably not lost on the service personnel suffering the attentions of real mosquitoes, breeding in the Nile Delta close at hand.

There was a definite stinging intention in the Italian-produced Mosquito anti-tank missile during the 1960s, and in the Mosquito handgun still produced by Swiss/German arms manufacturers SIG-Sauer.

MOSQUITOES FLY

It was in the development of aircraft that the mosquito brand really flourished. The Focke-Wulf Ta 154 Moskito was a German

Second-World-War aircraft that nearly was. It was designed as a fast night-fighter, the very time at which real mosquitoes were trying to bite sleepers, but after delays and losses it never became fully operational.

The Glasflügel Mosquito was a later German-manufactured glider. It first flew in 1976, but the name has more to do with exciting danger and skilful flying, rather than nuisance biting; it was part of a range that also included Hornet and Libelle (dragonfly).

In Britain, *the* mosquito is still the de Havilland DH.98 Mosquito fighter-bomber, first produced in 1940 and the hero of endless daring tales.[2] As well as being the fastest operational aircraft in the world, reaching nearly 640 km/h (400 mph), it was light and manoeuvrable. It was adapted for night-fighting and reconnaissance, but is best remembered as a tactical fast bomber, striking at small, difficult targets. Production ceased in 1950 and it was retired from the RAF in 1963, but the plane was so deeply etched into the British psyche that it continued to appear in books and films for many years to come. Biggles, the hero aviator of the long-running book series by W. E. Johns, regularly flew Mosquitoes. In *The Red Sea Sharks* (1956–8), Tintin helps counter a *coup d'état* in the fictional Arabian emirate of Khemed, which began following the illegal sale of several DH Mosquitoes to supporters of the obviously evil, pointy-nosed, pointy-bearded Sheikh Bab El Ehr. The planes make several appearances, once in blowing up the baddies in their own armoured car by accident, and again strafing Tintin and Captain Haddock aboard a dhow in the open sea.

Perhaps the best-known screen appearance of the bomber is in *633 Squadron* (1964), based on the novel by Frederick E. Smith, and chiefly remembered for the rousing theme tune by Ron Goodwin. The squadron of small-but-deadly mosquitoes

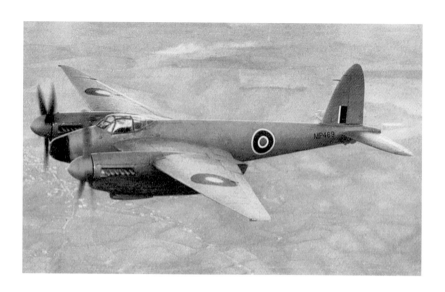

The epitome of stinging annoyance, tenacity and stealth, the de Havilland Mosquito fighter bomber, hero of endless tales of derring-do.

destroy a seemingly impregnable v-2 rocket fuel plant. They also have to destroy a Gestapo headquarters where a captured British airman is being tortured for information that could endanger the mission. For this sub-plot, the bomber takes on the mantle of targeted clinical assassin, a slightly darker reflection of the fly's original dangerous associations.

To my mind, the ethos of the de Havilland Mosquito is best portrayed in the later, better-acted, if rather unimaginatively named, *Mosquito Squadron* (1969). The film combines the nippy, eponymous aeroplanes with Barnes Wallis's bouncing bombs, smaller versions of those first meted out in *The Dambusters* back in 1954. *Mosquito Squadron* stars David McCallum as Squadron Leader Quint Munroe. Facing his commanding officer over a scale model of the pathetically small tunnel entrance to a Nazi research bunker, he's told: 'What we want you to do, Munroe, is to chuck a bomb in there. What do you say Munroe? What are the odds?' His reply, delivered deadpan, is: 'About the same as spitting in an air commodore's eye from a moving express train.'

Forty years on, the de Havilland Mosquito is still lauded as an aeronautic marvel. During early research for this book, a search for 'mosquito' on Amazon.com brought up a list of book titles where seventeen out of the top twenty were about this aeroplane, and only one was about the insect.

MOSQUITO STAMPS

There is the occasional scientifically positive appearance of mosquitoes in popular use. Insects feature regularly on stamps; usually bright butterflies and beetles, but mosquitoes are there, too. These are not celebrations of mosquito beauty, but of mosquito destruction.

The stamp design community all got together in 1962 to support the United Nations 'World United Against Malaria' campaign.[3] Italy's, of course, showed Giovanni Battista Grassi. The Cuban three showed *Plasmodium* parasites under the micro-scope, the mosquito vector and the chemical quinine. Jamaica was one of several countries showing insecticide spraying in action. Kenya's, rather disturbingly, shows a malaria victim looking very ill, with a horrid halo of the malaria infection cycle around his head. Mali's are the brightest, showing a series of informative treatment tableaux for the benefit of malaria-stricken letter-senders throughout the country. On a lighter note, the Vanuatu series depicts a horse rider (fund-raising charity races), an aeroplane ('on a mercy mission'), a bright new ambulance and a 'mosquito eradicated' sign. Hidden among the stamp designs is the occasional error of printing so highly valued by collectors. A whole series of Guinea stamps were printed with

From the simple to the decorative and informative, mosquito stamps emphasize the science and process behind malaria eradication.

EL MUNDO UNIDO CONTRA LA MALARIA

CLOROQUINA

Chinchona

CORREOS DE CUBA

3¢

MALARIA ERADICATION

35¢ SOLOMON ISLANDS

RÉPUBLIQUE DE
POSTE AÉRIENNE
GUINÉE
100F
LE MONDE UNI CONTRE LE PALUDISME

DE MUGGEN.
5. DE STEGOMYA.
LIEBIG PRODUKTEN : Verbeteren de spijsbereiding.
Nadruk verboden.   Uitleg op keerzijde.

DE MUGGEN.
6. DE VIJANDEN DER MUGGEN.
LIEBIG PRODUKTEN : Nuttig en praktisch.
Nadruk verboden.   Uitleg op keerzijde.

DE MUGGEN.
2. DE MALARIAMUG OF ANOPHELES.
LIEBIG PRODUKTEN : Knappen op.
Nadruk verboden.   Uitleg op keerzijde.

Mosquito-themed
collector's cards
show not just the
insects but protec-
tion methods, and
'helpful' predators in
the forms of birds,
fish, dragonflies
and salamanders.

IF THEY DON'T FIT,
THEY DON'T ENTER.
Anti insect net
for doors and windows.

Anti Insect Net **tesa**

The old magnified-to-the-proportions-of-a-monster trick is used to sell window screens.

the black mosquito upside down.[4] The legs-up death pose makes a silent, optimistic, and very moving, statement.

THE BRAND DEMISE

Of late, mosquito brands are cropping up everywhere as the mosquito name is misappropriated by manufacturers. But just as the real dangers of mosquitoes and mosquito-borne diseases are fading from memory in an affluent Western society, so too those cultural associations of persistence, pain and danger have become blurred. Today, the mosquito is also exciting, anarchic and cool. The Micro-Mosquito is a small, radio-controlled helicopter toy. There are Mosquito (and Moskito) motor scooters.

There are Moskito trainers. There are Mosquito branding companies, web designers, ad agencies, nightclubs, bars and clothing manufacturers. There are Mosquito fishing hooks, surgical forceps and kites. There is a Mosquito yo-yo.

All of these products are decorated with mosquito motifs, but from a marketing point of view, all that is required for 'brand recognition' is a generic winged insect, with a pointed beak at the front. Occasionally, the picture is stylized so far beyond any pretence of scientific accuracy, with the wrong number of wings or legs, that it verges on nonsense. But there is still something mosquitoish about it. Despite the tide of scientific advance, it seems that much of society is still using the vague Aristotelian notion of a pointy-faced *conops*, and is, by extension, failing to understand the difference between a mildly annoying biter and a deadly killer.

10 Mosquito Redux

In July 1983 Paul Braddon, landlord of the Royal Oak near Crawley in East Sussex, was taken ill with severe fever and hallucinations. He was diagnosed with cerebral malaria, the sudden and very dangerous form of the disease where the *Plasmodium falciparum* microbes have invaded the brain. If untreated, it is usually fatal within 72 hours. Every year thousands of holidaymakers unknowingly contract malaria while in the tropics; their symptoms are far milder than Mr Braddon's, but the fever and shakes are nevertheless unpleasant. Some have been careless (or reckless) with antimalarial prophylaxis (mistakenly associating malaria with murky swamps rather than smart holiday resorts); some have been unaware of local malarial dangers when they bought last-minute bargain holidays. The disease symptoms appear a few days later, but quinine treatment is usually swift and effective, and most victims are left with nothing worse than a cautionary tale of the dangers of not taking one's antimalarial medication when abroad.

However, Mr Braddon had made no such foreign trip. He had somehow been infected on home soil – the victim of a malaria-infected mosquito that had somehow stowed away on an airliner landing at London's Gatwick Airport, 9 km (6 m) away. It had escaped from its intercontinental transport and bitten him and a woman cycling past the pub, who also developed the disease.[1]

An infected mosquito's journey from somewhere in Africa to a rural pub in Sussex is more than remarkable. As well as surviving the jet travel of several thousand miles, it may also have had to face 'disinsection', the spraying of insecticide during the flight. Added to this, it seems unlikely that a mosquito could have flown the 9 km from the airport. Researchers who followed up the cases concluded that it could only have reached its final destination by car, probably continuing its stowaway transit with some of the aircrew that regularly visit the pub.[2]

These unfortunate people were but two of a long series of victims to succumb to 'airport' malaria. There are also clusters around Amsterdam's Schipol and Paris's Charles de Gaulle airports – both major hubs with large numbers of flights arriving from malarial foci. On the brink of writing this book, in December 2010, a 31-year-old woman from Duval (near Jacksonville), Florida was diagnosed with locally acquired falciparum malaria. Nobody yet knows how she got the disease, but this is a worry to the us medical authorities, Florida sitting, as it does, close to the tropical band of potentially falciparum-susceptible latitudes.

The stories were taken up by the media and, unfortunately, some were reported wildly out of proportion. Unlike other notifiable diseases such as measles or typhoid, the spread of malaria requires more than just an infectious agent arriving from the danger zone; it needs the complex interaction of parasite, human and mosquito, the complex interaction which made deciphering the disease so difficult in the first place.

Public health authorities in the us and uk could be excused for being slightly concerned. They knew there was a theoretical threat, even if they did not need the alarmist ideas put about by the *Daily Mail*, which suggested that such mosquitoes might establish a breeding colony of dangerous malaria-spreaders in the uk. This, of course, would be entirely unnecessary; several species of native British mosquitoes are quite capable of transmitting the vivax form of the disease. They did so right up to the end of the nineteenth century, during the time of ague. What concerns the medical profession is the spectre of repeating, or superseding, the events of 1917–21.

During and after the First World War men who had been fighting around the Mediterranean were repatriated in camps on the north Kent coast, at Sheppey and Grain. Many were sick with disease, including malaria, as well as suffering conventional war wounds. Here, surrounded by the low-lying watery meadows and salt marshes of the Medway, Swale and Thames, it was not long before the local mosquitoes picked up the blood-borne *Plasmodium* gametocytes and were incubating them in their own bodies, ready for the next stage of disease transmission. During the five years of the camps, 491 cases of malaria were detected in the resident local population, and children playing out of doors were especially prone.[3] The outbreak was only brought under control when cases were quarantined in special hospitals and local mosquito control measures were undertaken.

The invasion of malaria with a returning army was later to go from fact to fiction. In the April 1935 issue of *Amazing Stories*, H. M. Crimp wrote 'The Mosquito Army' using just this device. The science-fiction twist, in which the magazine revelled, was that Crimp's heroes find a way to remote-control the mosquitoes. This is a stroke of good luck, because the war with Russia is not going well. The boffins assemble a horde of mosquitoes, inoculate them with malaria and send them to bite the invading Russians. The attack withers, the invaders withdraw and the retreating soldiers take the malaria back to Russia, which collapses into disorder. Crimp is not just echoing modern history, his story also harks back to the invading Persians, who were blamed for introducing malaria into Greece in the fifth century BCE.

Lessons were learned in the real world, but even so, during the Second World War, 34 home-grown malaria cases were reported in Britain between 1941 and 1948. The last case of what was purported to be locally transmitted malaria in the UK was in 1953.[4]

THE RETURN OF BAD AIR

The greatest threat of malarial reinvasion comes, not from a few stowaway mosquitoes, but from the reversal of the factors that originally eradicated the disease – the dilution of malaria in the human population and the destruction of mosquito breeding sites. In other words, malaria could make a comeback if there were changes in local population density, immigration of non-medicated, malaria-carrying humans (as happened in Kent in 1917–21) and an increase in the local mosquito breeding grounds. All of these three factors combine to produce their effects, but it is the presence of suitable mosquito breeding habitats that is arguably the greatest component in the equation.

Today, the fens and meres of East Anglia are faint echoes of the once magnificent area of quagmire that covered huge parts of Lincolnshire, Cambridgeshire, Norfolk and Suffolk. They are home to endangered populations of the English swallowtail butterfly, fen orchid, bittern, and a whole host of other threatened plant and animal species, which contracted as the land was drained for agriculture. They were not the only things to decline in the area – mosquitoes, too, were reduced, as their breeding sites were destroyed in the nineteenth and twentieth centuries by the relatively easy landscape adjustment of simply digging ditches. An opposite effect was noted during the Dark Ages, when large tracts of Europe became uninhabitable because of malaria after they were lost from agriculture, possibly connected with successive waves of lower global temperatures and resulting crop failures.[5]

Malarial decline was also linked to rapid changes in the population structure of the area. As the crop fields expanded, and with increasing mechanization, there was a corresponding depopulation, as rural workers migrated to cities during the Industrial Revolution. This depopulation effectively diluted the reservoir of malaria sufferers to the point where any surviving mosquitoes were not picking up infected blood any more.

Similar combinations of changing mosquito habitat and local human population densities controlled malaria epidemics elsewhere in the world. Before the Anglo–American War of 1812, the swampy region around the Rideau and Cataraqui Rivers in Ontario, Canada, were sparsely populated and malaria was virtually unknown. In case of future military conflict, the British government built the Rideau Canal linking Ottawa and Kingston. Malaria was soon rife among construction workers. The mosquitoes had always been present, but the disease parasites were possibly brought in by soldiers. The waterway was opened in 1832, and although malaria remained established in the area for many years, it had vanished by 1900.[6] No doubt, quinine use had some effect here, but the drug was still relatively expensive for mass pharmaceutical attack on the parasite. When construction work was completed, the human population declined to a residual rural level, effectively diluting the disease concentration in the area. Habitat alteration would also have an effect. With the canal now running across the landscape, control of water through ditches and sluices had transformed the previous labyrinthine network of shallow pools (ideal mosquito breeding grounds) into a managed network of neat drainage ditches and dykes.

The Pontine Marshes around Rome had begun being drained centuries ago, beginning with Julius Caesar, but the most important works were set in motion in the 1930s. Earth-moving machinery, pumping stations and public awareness effectively vanquished malaria in the area. But what was done would later be undone. During the Nazi retreat through Italy in 1943, the German army flooded 81,000 ha (200,000 acres) of this reclaimed land to impede the allied advance. Malaria cases erupted within a year, causing some commentators to brand the action as biological warfare and bioterrorism.[7]

GLOBAL WARMING

In *The Drowned World* (1962) J. G. Ballard contemplates a future where increased solar radiation has melted the polar ice caps and left the major cities of the developed world as flooded lagoons. Set in London in the year 2145, the novel describes tropical temperatures, apocalyptic flooding and the enhanced evolution of plants and animals. The characters suffer as a result of the burning radiation, and malaria is back. The discovery in the 1980s of the threadbare state of the ozone layer and the later realization that carbon dioxide emissions were leading to climate change made Ballard's story disconcertingly prescient. Flooding is one of the most pressing threats from both of these phenomena. Estimates vary, but sea levels are set to rise by anything from 1 to 50 m (3–165 ft) during the next century. Even at the most conservative end of this panic spectrum, many low-lying areas of the world will suffer unstoppable inundation, and the creation of huge, brackish swamps favoured by mosquitoes. Already in the UK, the Environment Agency is preparing to offer up coastal areas of Sussex, Kent and East Anglia to the rising tides. These are precisely the regions where vivax malaria was historically present.

Concerns are sometimes voiced that increasing world temperatures will increase the spread and penetration of tropical diseases. When bluetongue virus (a serious foot-and-mouth-like disease of sheep) appeared spontaneously in northern Europe in 2006 and in Britain in 2007, its arrival was traced to vectors (biting midges, *Culicoides obsoletus*) that were being blown north from Africa and the Mediterranean and were surviving during the hot summer. Higher global temperatures might seem to encourage the movement, and survival further north, of tropical-disease-spreading mosquitoes. Intuitive though this increasing temperature model may be, things are never quite this simple.[8] For example, over the last five years, bloodsucking ticks have also been moving north through Scandinavia. These biting arachnids are second only to mosquitoes in their importance as disease vectors, spreading Lyme disease and boutonneuse fever among others, but their movement in Sweden is linked more to increasing numbers of deer (their prime food source) rather than temperature.

It is true that one of the main limits on the more deadly falciparum malaria is that it needs a higher temperature for development in the mosquito, and cannot develop below about 20°C (68°F). The vivax form of the disease is much less sensitive, and the usual figures quoted are temperatures above 15°C (59°F) for one month for it to successfully propagate inside its insect host. Vivax can also sustain itself in a cool geographical region because it has that latent liver phase. The human carrier appears to be in remission, only for some trigger to release the blood parasites again after many months, ready for a summer mosquito to sup its fill.

To some extent, the temperature is irrelevant. Mosquitoes occur right up to the Arctic Circle, and overwinter in egg, larva, pupa or adult stage even under feet of snow. Vivax malaria, ague, was able to cope quite happily in Europe during the little ice age; this was the period from the sixteenth to the nineteenth century when winters in Europe were noticeably much harder than in the medieval warm period which finished about 1300.[9] Glaciers around the world grew rather than shrank, Bruegel the Elder was busy painting peasant snow scenes and there were regular frost fairs on the frozen Thames. Meanwhile, Shakespeare was poking fun at Aguecheek, and everyone from Defoe to Dickens was using ague motifs whenever one of their characters required the shakes. Malaria did not need a tropical, even mild, climate, it just needed mosquitoes and an ague-ridden populace. What did for the disease in Europe and North America was the change in the rural economy: depopulation, linked to the Industrial Revolution, removing the ague-infected humans, and land increasingly drained, removing the mosquitoes.[10] Cheap quinine was the final nail in the malarial coffin. In the USA at least, DDT was, after all, complete overkill; as US historian Margaret Humphreys put it: like 'kicking a dying dog'.[11]

MOSQUITO COMEBACK

The chances of ague or malaria returning to the developed world are, according to most scientists, remote. The downward trend of the disease is still relatively fast, and any backtracking is unlikely to pose a significant threat. Even in tropical countries with endemic malaria, transmission is still declining in most places. Insecticide-treated bed nets and antimalarial drugs are still having a positive effect. But not all is forward advance.

In 1963 there were just seventeen cases of malaria reported in Ceylon (Sri Lanka), a country once wracked with the disease. Active DDT spraying, regular blood tests, cheap quinine and a successful public awareness campaign had served up a promising result and a country free of the disease seemed to be on the horizon. But by 1969 malaria was returning unimpeded and there were over half a million cases. What had gone wrong?

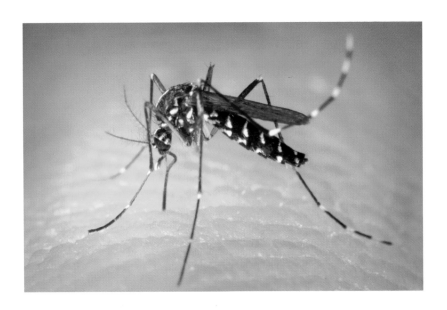

The Asian tiger mosquito, *Aedes albopictus*, has been moved all around the world in the rain slops of second-hand tyres.

Perhaps a blasé attitude was setting in. Chemical spraying had all but stopped in the early 1960s as money-saving cutbacks were brought in too early. There was a chaotic logjam of blood tests awaiting examination and many cases went undetected and therefore untreated. When panic DDT spraying was started again, after a poorly concerted interim programme, the carrier mosquitoes were found to have developed chemical resistance to it. Sprayers switched to the more expensive malathion, but the mosquitoes already had the upper hand. Worse, the proportion of the more deadly falciparum strain had increased from almost zero to 16 per cent. This was very bad news.[12]

As if a possible escalation of malaria was not bad enough, other mosquito-borne diseases are also on the increase across the world. This time, it is not just movement of people bringing in the disease, but movement of mosquitoes, too. The Asian tiger mosquito, *Aedes albopictus*, is a prettily marked black-and-white species, native to Southeast Asia. It is a particularly aggressive species, biting during the day, and is known to spread dengue fever and West Nile virus. There was great consternation when it was found a hemisphere away from its native range, in Texas, in 1985. It also turned up in Brazil, Mexico, Argentina, Cuba and in 1990 reached Italy. Eventually, its mode of international transport was identified – larvae were being transported via the water slops in cargos of used car tyres.[13] Tyres are expensive to manufacture new; second-hand tyres are cheap and easy to transport and can sit for days or weeks on the dockside in all weathers, plus there is a worldwide market in reusing and remoulding them.

The mosquito is now well established in southern Europe and most of the southeastern USA, and is making inroads into West Africa and South America. In 2005–6, in a startling echo of the Mauritius malaria outbreak of 1866, *Aedes albopictus* was responsible for an epidemic of Chikungunya fever on the Indian Ocean island of Réunion, where a quarter of a million people fell ill and 250 died.[14] Australia and New Zealand are on full mosquito-alert to prevent it becoming established, but it has already reached New Guinea and the Torres Strait Islands. It has not yet reached the UK, but there is every expectation that it will arrive soon.

And things can get still worse. We live, apparently, in an unscrupulous and criminal world. Something in the order of 10–15 per cent of antimalarial drugs on the global market are believed to be fakes.[15] Harry Lime would be rubbing his hands with glee. When Orson Welles played this disreputable character in his film *The Third Man* (1949), it was adulterated antibiotics he was peddling. If the storyline is ever taken up for a Bollywood blockbuster, it will be fake quinine that the antihero is foisting on to a desperate and unsuspecting public.

11 The Mosquito Legacy

It is now over a century since the ins and outs of the mosquito bite and its associated parasites were first elucidated, but malaria still haunts us. Reported numbers range widely, but a safe estimate is given in the latest (2009) figures from the World Health Organization (WHO).[1] Some news is good. In Africa, eleven countries showed a greater than 50 per cent malaria reduction 'in recent years'. This is mainly due to the 290 million insecticide-impregnated bed nets issued to families in sub-Saharan Africa over the last decade. But there are still 106 malaria-endemic countries and areas in the world, and an estimated 225 million malaria sufferers, although this is down on the 244 million recorded in 2005. The financial burden of malaria is still massive, estimated to be 20 per cent of gross domestic product in some countries, not just from deaths, but from chronic and debilitating sickness. And, of course, malaria is still a fatal disease. During 2009, the WHO estimated that 781,000 people died of malaria. Again, this is down from the 985,000 deaths estimated in 2000, but is still the ghastly equivalent of five Boeing 747s crashing every day of the year.

Health charities continue to push for greater awareness and to raise funds. And just as Mr Moore Hogarth found in the 1920s, celebrity endorsement is worth its weight in quinine. Victoria Beckham sported a special mosquito ring designed by Stephen Webster, which was sold to benefit the Malaria No

More organization. Actress Sharon Stone made headlines when she spoke out at the World Economic Forum meeting in Switzerland in 2005. She offered Tanzanian president Benjamin Mkapa US$10,000 for bed nets, and according to news reports raised US $1 million from the audience within minutes.[2] Save the Children used their 'celebrity sponsors' – TV presenter Davina McCall, musician Fran Healey and journalist and broadcaster Mariella Frostrup – to launch World Malaria Day (25 April) in 2008, photographing them posing in swathes of mosquito netting.[3] The celebrity glitter is often necessary to get over the fact that malaria is not very newsworthy. It occurs in other countries, affects other people, and the photo opportunities are not exactly glamorous.

One of the problems of trying to get malaria noticed by the international press is that, over a century on from that momentous year, 1897, our means of coping with both fly and parasite have changed little. We keep poisoning the waterholes, and we poison the parasite with quinine, or synthetic substitutes. But there is still a long way to go.

Biodiversity is a powerful buzzword, and the idea of eradicating a species sits ill with notions of conservation. Would it really matter if mosquitoes ceased to exist? In a thoughtful article in *Nature* examining just this question, Janet Fang was offered the conclusion that there is nothing mosquitoes 'do' (pollination, recycling organic matter, food for predators and so on) that other insects could not do instead – apart from transmit malaria.[4] Consequently if there were no mosquitoes, there would be no malaria, and there would be more humans.

Thankfully, this total wipeout scenario is not entirely necessary. If enough mosquitoes can be killed and enough malaria-suffering humans treated, there comes a tipping point at which transmission no longer occurs and malaria collapses. But even this 'second best' option is a tough target.

The seemingly insurmountable obstacle that we cannot quite overcome is the combination of incomprehensible mosquito numbers and the logistical nightmare of trying to treat a complex and highly mobile human population. Because they breed so quickly, a few surviving mosquitoes can repopulate within weeks, and they are liable to be the insecticide-resistant ones. There is also uneasiness about what this destruction might mean to the wider environment, to non-target organisms, and the spectre of a tropics-wide 'silent spring'. It is also difficult to administer the intensive medication necessary to rid (or reduce) an entire human population of the malaria blood parasites. All it takes is for one sick person to move from one area to another and the disease is taken into another town or country that may have been previously cleared of the disease, and the cycle starts all over again. We have new insecticides (including mosquito-killing bacteria) and powerful drugs, but this is still the old-fashioned strategy of the mosquito squads. Is there no other way?

Polio, measles and rubella are in terminal decline, and in the case of smallpox, extinction has been achieved. All this has been by immunization. A vaccine against *Plasmodium* is now the holy grail of malaria research. The problem with malaria is that, although *Plasmodium* is a simple, single-celled animalcule, it is still vastly more complex than bacteria or viruses; developing a usable vaccine is far from straightforward. Also, *Plasmodium* constantly changes its surface chemicals, as if evolution has gone into overdrive. A conventional vaccine against one particular strain becomes obsolete before it can be put to use. Nevertheless, work continues.

Bill Gates, chairman of Microsoft and some-time richest man in the world, has been pushing for this vaccine project to be taken very seriously. At a well-publicized conference in Long Beach, California, in 2009, Gates spoke on malaria. He joked that more money was spent on baldness drugs than on a disease that kills roughly a million people a year. Baldness is a terrible and debilitating condition that afflicts rich men, hence the pressing enthusiasm driving this line of research.

To give his audience a taste of mosquito misery, Gates released a container of live mosquitoes into the auditorium: 'There's no reason only poor people should have the experience.' It did what it was intended to do; it caught the media's attention, even though they rather blew it up into a 'cloud' or a 'swarm' of mosquitoes. Bill Gates is obviously moved by the world's malarial malaise and the Bill and Melinda Gates Foundation funds many malaria projects. In November 2010 the foundation gave US$50 million to the Liverpool School of Tropical Medicine. At the moment Bill Gates is known as the man who got a personal computer onto almost every desk in the world. If he can help get a dose of malaria vaccine into everyone living in the malarial tropics, it will be a much more fitting and honourable epitaph.

As I have argued, it is one of the consequences of losing malaria in developed countries that the weighty concern and immediacy of the disease has also been rather lost. And with the concern, all that hard-told and hard-learned knowledge vaporizes, too. All those key facts pressed on an eager world by the likes of Walt Disney and Dr. Seuss, about the *Anopheles* body position (45-degree angle, tail stuck up in the air), about breeding cycles in gutters and puddles and litter, and about disease transmission through infected saliva (not regurgitated blood), fade, and what is left is a kind of medieval mosquito bestiary, a hodgepodge of mosquito half-truths and folklore. Mosquitoes are far from gone in the world, but the mosquito menace is much reduced in many Western minds.

In *101 Things to Do with a Mosquito* (2005), cartoonist Ed Fischer suggests everything from using them as darts to flattening them as bookmarks. Some of his ideas have already been used; 'smooshed mosquito art' made an appearance in Atlanta, Georgia. This looks familiar; a man standing behind his lectern holds up a jar of the flies, and demands: 'If you don't listen to me – I'll release these mosquitoes.' Not one of the cartoons makes reference to malaria or disease.

Larson, again, has a better go at it. Even though there is still no mention of the deadly parasites within, the sinister shadow cast by these flies is used to good effect in his gloomy night-time cartoon showing the husband and wife couple in their bed. 'Dang it! Doris! Hit the light! . . . I think there's a mosquito after me.' There is, it's hiding in the corner, and it's as big as an ox. Just as in Walt Disney's wartime public information film, *The Winged Scourge*, Larson's mosquito is magnified to the proportions of a monster. The personal attention of a giant mosquito familiar is funny. The impersonal attention of malaria-infected mosquito hordes is not funny. But this is the image of the killer insect we should try and keep in our minds if we want to keep mosquitoes and malaria in perspective.

Malaria remains the greatest human killer in the world, but even the organizations promoting its understanding and control can still get it wrong. Christian Aid, in a recent series of UK newspaper adverts to encourage readers to sponsor antimalarial bed nets, showed a sad, malaria-infected child; they also pictured a large, but obviously non-malarial, mosquito (without its rear end stuck in the air at a 45-degree angle). Does it matter? As long as they get the £1 text message donation they're after, perhaps not. But if they can't get a basic biological fact right at one end of the money tree, it does rather raise questions about whether they know what they're doing at the other end, where it matters what sort of mosquito bites you. Where it is, quite literally, a matter of life and death.

Timeline of the Mosquito

c. 200 MYA	100–76 MYA	*c.* 1323 BCE	*c.* 1300–1200 BCE	*c.* 500 BCE
Estimated appearance of the first true mosquitoes	The earliest known fossils of mosquitoes trapped in amber	Tutankhamun died, possibly as a result of a broken leg exacerbated by malaria infection	Biblical plague of flies – most likely mosquitoes	Invading Persians are blamed for the introduction of malaria to ancient Greece

1860s	1866	1877	1880–1884	1881
Paris green is used for the first time as an insecticide 	Malaria vector *Anopheles gambiae* is accidentally introduced to Mauritius, causing a huge epidemic	Patrick Manson shows that the filarial worm responsible for elephantiasis is incubated in the bodies of mosquitoes	Charles Laveran sees moving specks, the protozoan responsible for malaria, in sufferers' blood 	Carlos Finlay suggests that yellow fever is spread by mosquitoes

1939	1943	1953	1963	1983
The insect-killing properties of DDT are discovered	Walt Disney's *The Winged Scourge*, an anti-mosquito and malaria-awareness cartoon	The last case of locally transmitted malaria in the UK	Malaria is almost eradicated from Sri Lanka, but a resurgence occurs because controls are lifted too early	Two people living downwind of London's Gatwick Airport contract malaria from a stowaway *Anopheles* mosquito

c. 450 CE	16th century	1583	1740	1858
The eve of the fall of Rome, possibly linked to the arrival of more deadly falciparum malaria	Spanish colonizers 'discover' that stewed cinchona bark cures malaria	The word 'mosquito' first appears in the English language	The word 'malaria' is used for the first time in the English language	Alfred Russel Wallace, laid up 'under a cold fit of ague' (malaria) writes his letter-essay on evolution to Charles Darwin

1882–9	1897	1900	1901–1910
French efforts to build the Panama Canal fail because of mosquito-borne disease	Three key discoveries: Ronald Ross identifies the parasites of bird malaria in mosquito bodies; Giovanni Grassi successfully infects a healthy person with malaria via a mosquito bite; and Robert Koch demonstrates that quinine destroys malaria parasites in human blood	Walter Reed finally proves that yellow fever is spread by mosquitoes	Frederick Theobald's four-volume *Monograph on the Culicidae* is published

1985	1993	2009	2010
The Asian tiger mosquito, *Aedes albopictus*, vector of dengue and West Nile virus, is introduced into the USA from the Far East in second-hand car-tyre rain slops	Dinosaur blood preserved in mosquitoes trapped in amber is the plot basis for the film *Jurassic Park*	Bill Gates releases live mosquitoes into the auditorium in California where he is speaking in support of malaria research	The Bill and Melinda Gates Foundation gives US\$50 million to the Liverpool School of Tropical Medicine (founded in 1898, the oldest specialist tropical medicine research centre in the world)

References

1 WILL IT BITE?

1 I. C. Beavis, *Insects and Other Invertebrates in Classical Antiquity* (Exeter, 1988), pp. 229–36.

2 J. O. Westwood, *The Entomologist's Text-Book. An Introduction to the Natural History, Structure, Physiology and Classification of Insects* (London, 1838), p. 17.

3 P. Marren and R. Mabey, *Bugs Britannica* (London, 2010), p. 302.

4 Beavis, *Insects and Other Invertebrates*, p. 229.

5 Ibid., p. 234.

6 J. Ray, *The Wisdom of God Manifested in the Works of Creation: In Two Parts viz. the Heavenly Bodies, Elements, Meteors, Fossils, Vegetables, Animals (Beasts, Birds, Fishes, and Insects)* . . . [1691], facsimile reprint (London, 1826), pp. 84–5.

7 G. O. Poinar et al., '*Paleoculicis minutus* (Diptera: Culicidae) n. gen., n. sp., from Cretaceous Canadian Amber, with a Summary of Described Fossil Mosquitoes', *Acta Geologica Hispanica*, 35 (2000), pp. 119–28; A. Borkent and D. A. Grimaldi, 'The Earliest Fossil Mosquito (Diptera: Culicidae), in mid-Cretaceous Burmese Amber', *Annals of the Entomological Society of America*, 97 (2004), pp. 882–8.

8 E. Calvo et al., 'The Salivary Gland Transcriptome of the Neotropical Malaria Vector *Anopheles darlingi* Reveals Accelerated Evolution of Genes Relevant to Hematophagy', *BMC Genomics*, 10 (2009), p. 57.

9 S. Spitaleri et al., 'Genotyping of Human DNA Recovered from

Mosquitoes Found on a Crime Scene', in *Progress in Forensic Genetics*, 11: *Proceedings of the 21st International ISFG Congress Held in Ponta Delgada, The Azores, Portugal, between 13 and 16 September 2005* (2006), pp. 574–6.

10 J. D. Gillett, *Mosquitoes*, The World Naturalist Series (London, 1971).

2 WHY DRINK BLOOD?

1 Twinn et al., 1948, quoted in J. D. Gillett, *Mosquitoes*, The World Naturalist Series (London, 1971), p. 58.

2 J. Hogg, *The Microscope: Its History, Construction, and Application: Being a Familiar Introduction to the Use of the Instrument, and the Study of Microscopical Science* (London, 1854), pp. 598–9.

3 M. W. Service, 'Observations on Feeding and Oviposition in Some British Mosquitoes', *Entomologia Experimentalis et Applicata*, 11 (1968), pp. 277–85.

4 John Updike, 'Mosquito', *New Yorker* (11 June 1960), p. 32.

5 D. James, *Mosquito: An Omnilingual Nosferatu Pictomunication Novel* (Marietta, GA, 2005).

6 Service, 'Observations on Feeding and Oviposition'.

7 D. H. Lawrence, *Pansies: A Selection* (n.p., 1929).

8 D. H. Lawrence, *Birds, Beasts and Flowers* (London, 1923).

9 F. Adcock and J. Simms, eds, *The Oxford Book of Creatures* (Oxford, 1995), p. 260.

3 PEST PROPORTIONS

1 G. Morge, 'Entomology in the Western World in Antiquity and in Medieval Times', in *History of Entomology*, ed. R. F. Smith, T. E. Mittler and C. N. Smith (Palo Alto, CA, 1973), p. 67.

2 Ibid., p. 57.

3 Z. Syed and W. S. Leal, 'Acute Olfactory Response of *Culex* Mosquitoes to a Human- and Bird-derived Attractant', *Proceedings of the National Academy of Sciences USA*, 106 (2009), pp. 18,803–8.

4 Pedro Teixeira, *The Travels of Pedro Teixeira; with His 'Kings of*

Marmuz', and Extracts from His 'Kings of Persia', trans. W. F. Sinclair,
with further notes and introduction by D. Fergusson
(London, 1902).

5 Brian Hocking, quoted in J. D. Gillett, *Mosquitoes*, The World
Naturalist Series (London, 1971), p. 149.

6 Ibid., p. 80.

7 O. Sotavalta, 'Recordings of High Wing-stroke and Thoracic
Vibration Frequency in Some Midges', *The Biological Bulletin*, 104
(1953), pp. 439–44.

8 Morge, 'Entomology in the Western World', p. 57.

9 V. Aardema, *Why Mosquitoes Buzz in People's Ears: A West African
Tale* (New York, 1975).

4 MOSQUITO PLACES

1 I. C. Beavis, *Insects and Other Invertebrates in Classical Antiquity*
(Exeter, 1988), p. 235.

2 Ibid., pp. 231–2.

3 G. Morge, 'Entomology in the Western World in Antiquity and in
Medieval Times', in *History of Entomology*, ed. R. F. Smith, T. E.
Mittler and C. N. Smith (Palo Alto, CA, 1973), p. 67.

4 J. R. Harris, *An Angler's Entomology* (London, 1952).

5 S. A. Allan, J. F. Day and J. D. Edman, 'Visual Ecology of Biting
Flies', *Annual Review of Entomology*, XXXII (1987), pp. 297–314.

6 A. Thwaite, *Glimpses of the Wonderful; The Life of Philip Henry
Gosse, 1810–1888* (London, 2002), p. 70.

7 J. Banks, *Journal of the Right Hon. Sir Joseph Banks during Captain
Cook's First Voyage in H.M.S. 'Endeavour' in 1768–71 to Terra del
Fuego, Otahite, New Zealand, Australia, The Dutch East Indies, etc.*
(London, 1896), p. 273.

8 N. Moore, 'Introduction', in C. Waterton, *Wanderings in South
America, The North-West of the United States, and the Antilles, in the
Years 1812, 1816, 1820 and 1824* (London, 1891), p. 49.

9 A. R. Wallace, *A Narrative of Travels on the Amazon and Rio Negro,
with an Account of the Native Tribes and Observations on the*

Climate, Geology, and Natural History of the Amazon Valley
(London, 1853), p. 11.

10 Ibid., p. 137.

11 Ibid., p. 99.

12 Ibid., pp. 99–100.

13 A. R. Wallace, *The Malay Archipelago: The Land of the Urang-Utan
and the Bird of Paradise. A Narrative of Travel with Studies of Man
and Nature* (London, 1869), chapter 31.

14 Ibid.

15 Wallace, *The Malay Archipelago*, pp. 338–9.

16 Ibid., p. 391.

17 From a letter written by Wallace. 'How Was Wallace Led to the
Discovery of Natural Selection?', at http://people.wku.edu/
charles.smith/index1.htm, accessed 1 November 2011. He also
refers to this, using slightly different words, in his autobiography:
A. R. Wallace, *My Life: A Record of Events and Opinions* (London,
1905).

18 A. R. Wallace, 'On the Tendency of Varieties to Depart
Indefinitely from the Original Type', *Journal of the Proceedings of
the Linnean Society*, 18 (2nd series; 1858), pp. 53–62.

5 THE PARASITE WITHIN

1 W. R. Dawson, 'A Norfolk Vicar's Charm Against Ague', *Original
Papers of the Norfolk and Norwich Archaeological Society*, 24 (1932),
pp. 233–8.

2 Z. Hawass, Y. Z. Gad, S. Ismail et al., 'Ancestry and Pathology in
King Tutankhamun's Family', *Journal of the American Medical
Association*, CCCIII (2010), pp. 638–47.

3 J.L.A. Webb, Jr, *Humanity's Burden: A Global History of Malaria*
(New York, 2009), pp. 59–60.

4 J. D. Gillett, *Mosquitoes*, The World Naturalist Series (London,
1971), p. 193.

5 Ibid., p. 194.

6 I. C. Beavis, *Insects and Other Invertebrates in Classical Antiquity*

(Exeter, 1988), p. 234.

7   Ibid.

8   Webb, *Humanity's Burden*, p. 67.

9   Gillett, *Mosquitoes*, p. 193.

10 L. J. Bruce-Chwatt, 'John MacCulloch, M.D., F.R.S. (1773–1835)'
    (the precursor of the discipline of malariology), *Medical History*,
    21 (1977), pp. 156–65.

11 J. MacCulloch, *Malaria: an Essay on the Production and
    Propagation of This Poison, and on the Nature and Localities of the
    Places by Which It Is Produced: with an Enumeration of the Diseases
    Caused by it, and of the Means of Preventing or Diminishing Them,
    Both at Home and in the Naval and Military Service* (London, 1827).

12 P. Reiter, 'From Shakespeare to Defoe: Malaria in England in the
    Little Ice Age', *Emerging Infectious Diseases*, VI (2000), pp. 1–11.

13 D. Defoe, *Tour through the Eastern Counties of England, 1722*
    (London, 1888).

14 A. Nicholls, 'Fenland Ague in the Nineteenth Century', *Medical
    History*, XLIV (2000), pp. 513–30.

15 Ibid.

16 Ibid.

17 Gillett, *Mosquitoes*, p. 195.

18 Ibid.

19 Ibid., p. 154.

20 Ibid.

21 A. von Humboldt and A. Bonplan, *Personal Narrative of Travels
    to the Equinoctal Regions of America During the Years 1799–1804*;
    written in French by A. von Humboldt, trans. and ed. T. Ross
    (London, 1852), vol. III, pp. 284–5.

22 Ibid., p. 285.

23 Ibid.

24 Ibid., pp. 288–9.

25 D. Livingstone, *Missionary Travels and Researches in South Africa;
    Including a Sketch of Sixteen Years' Residence in the Interior . . .*
    (London, 1857).

26 R. W. Boyce, *Mosquito or Man? The Conquest of the Tropical World*,

3rd edn (London, 1910), pp. 24–5.

27 L. O. Howard, *A History of Applied Entomology (Somewhat Anecdotal)*, (Washington, DC, 1930), p. 470.

28 Boyce, *Mosquito or Man?*, p. 35.

29 C. B. Philip and L. E. Rozeboom, 'Medico-veterinary Entomology: A Generation of Progress', in *History of Entomology*, ed. R. F. Smith, T. E. Mittler and C. N. Smith (Palo Alto, CA, 1973), p. 355.

30 Ibid., p. 356.

31 Howard, *A History of Applied Entomology*, p. 470.

32 Webb, *Humanity's Burden*, pp. 128–9.

33 Howard, *A History of Applied Entomology*, p. 482.

34 Ibid., p. 471.

35 Ibid., pp. 483, 491

36 Boyce, *Mosquito or Man?*, pp. 43–4.

37 F. J. Ayala, A. A. Scalante and S. M. Rich, 'Evolution of *Plasmodium* and the Recent Origin of the World Populations of *Plasmodium falciparum*', *Parassitologia*, 41 (1999), pp. 55–68.

38 Webb, *Humanity's Burden*.

39 R. F. Burton, *Personal Narrative of a Pilgrimage to Al-Madinah and Meccah*, memorial edn (London, 1893).

40 R. Sallares and S. Gomzi, 'Biomolecular Archaeology of Malaria', *Ancient Biomolecules*, III (2001), pp. 195–213.

6 THE MARCH OF PROGRESS

1 R. W. Boyce, *Mosquito or Man? The Conquest of the Tropical World*, 3rd edn (London, 1910), pp. 158–214.

2 P. D. Curtin, 'Medical Knowledge and Urban Planning in Tropical Africa', *The American Historical Review*, XC (1985), pp. 594–613.

3 R. E. Cheeseman, *In Unknown Arabia* (London, 1926), pp. 83–4.

4 P. G. Shute, '*Culex molestus*', *Transactions of the Royal Entomological Society of London*, CII (1951), pp. 380–82.

5 K. Byrne and R. A. Nichols, '*Culex pipiens* in London Underground Tunnels: Differentiation between Surface and Subterranean Populations', *Heredity*, LXXXII (1999), pp. 7–15.

6 G.H.F. Nuttall, L. Cobbett and T. Strangeways-Pigg, 'Studies in Relation to Malaria: 1. The Geographical Distribution of *Anopheles* in Relation to the Former Distribution of Ague in England', *Journal of Hygiene (London)*, 1 (1901), pp. 4–44.

7 W. D. Lang, *A Map Showing the Known Distribution in England and Wales of the Anopheline Mosquitoes, with Explanatory Text and Notes* (London, 1918).

8 G.H.F. Nuttall and A. E. Shipley, 'Studies in Relation to Malaria: 2. The Structure and Biology of *Anopheles* (*Anopheles maculipennis*), the Egg and Larva', *Journal of Hygiene (London)*, 1 (1901), pp. 45–77.

9 C. B. Philip and L. E. Rozeboom, 'Medico-veterinary Entomology: a Generation of Progress', in *History of Entomology*, ed. R. F. Smith, T. E. Mittler and C. N. Smith (Palo Alto, CA, 1973), p. 335.

10 Boyce, *Mosquito or Man?*, pp. 3, 11.

11 Ibid., pp. 4, 31.

12 A. Moore Hogarth, *British Mosquitoes and How to Eliminate Them* (London, 1928), p. 20.

13 Ibid., p. 46

14 M. Bock, 'Disease and Medicine', in *Joseph Conrad in Context*, ed. H. Simmons (Cambridge, 2009), pp. 124–31.

15 K. R. Snow, *Mosquitoes*, Naturalists' Handbooks 14 (Slough, 1990).

7 THE THEATRE OF WAR

1 R. Wallace, ed., *Eleanor Ormerod, LLD, Economic Entomologist: Autobiography and Correspondence* (London, 1904).

2 J.M.F. Clark, *Bugs and the Victorians* (New Haven, CT, 2009), p. 150.

3 Wallace, *Eleanor Ormerod*, p. 207.

4 M. Farr, *Tintin: The Complete Companion* (London, 2001).

5 J.L.A. Webb, Jr, *Humanity's Burden: A Global History of Malaria* (New York, 2009), p. 93.

6 A. W. Haggis, 'Fundamental Errors in the History of Cinchona', *Bulletin of the History of Medicine*, x (1941), pp. 568–87.

7 F. Rocco, *The Miraculous Fever Tree: The Cure that Changed the*

World (London, 2003).

8 Webb, *Humanity's Burden*, pp. 92–126.

9 M. Leaf, *This is Ann: She's Dying to Meet You* (Washington, DC, 1943).

10 This dextrous and chemically uplifting limerick by Dr D. D. Perrin of Deakin University, Western Australia, is widely credited on the internet, but a definitive first publication date and location could not be found.

8 ENVIRONMENTAL CHAOS

1 C. B. Philip and L. E. Rozeboom, 'Medico-veterinary Entomology: a Generation of Progress', in *History of Entomology*, ed. R. F. Smith, T. E. Mittler and C. N. Smith (Palo Alto, CA, 1973), p. 356.

2 R. Carson, *Silent Spring* (Boston, MA, 1962), ch. 1.

3 A. S. Cooke, 'Shell Thinning in Avian Eggs by Environmental Pollutants', *Environmental Pollution*, IV (1973), pp. 85–152.

4 L. Lear, 'Afterword', in R. Carson, *Silent Spring* (London, 1998; rep. 1999).

5 G. Davidson, 'Insecticide Resistance in *Anopheles gambiae* Giles: a Case of Simple Mendelian Inheritance', *Nature*, CLXXVIII (195 pp. 861–4.

9 THE MOSQUITO BRAND

1 S. S. Cohen, *Yankee Sailors in British Gaols: Prisoners of War at Forton and Mill, 1777–1783* (Cranbury, NJ, 1995).

2 M. Bowman, *de Havilland Mosquito*, Crowood Aviation Series (Marlborough, 2005).

3 www.malariastamps.com, accessed 1 November 2011.

4 Ibid.

10 MOSQUITO REDUX

1 D. Whitfield et al., 'Two Cases of *falciparum* Malaria Acquired in Britain', *British Medical Journal*, CCLXXXIX (1984), pp. 1,607–09.

2 C. F. Curtis and G. B. White, '*Plasmodium falciparum* Transmission in England: Entomological Data Relative to Cases in 1983', *Journal of Tropical Hygiene and Medicine*, 14 (1984), pp. 275–82.

3 P. G. Shute, 'A Review of Indigenous Malaria in Great Britain after the War of 1939–1945, Compared with the Corresponding Period after the 1914–1918 War (with some observations of the aetiology)', *Monthly Bulletin of the Ministry of Health and Public Health Laboratory Service*, 8 (1949), pp. 2–9.

4 G. S. Crockett and K. Simpson, 'Malaria in Neighbouring Londoners', *British Medical Journal*, II (1953), pp. 1,141–2.

5 W.H.S. Jones, *Malaria: a Neglected Factor in the History of Greece and Rome* (Cambridge, 1907).

6 Ken W. Watson, 'Malaria: A Rideau Mythconception', at www.rideau-info.com, accessed 1 November 2011.

7 F. M. Snowden, *The Conquest of Malaria: Italy, 1900–1962* (New Haven, CT, 2006), pp. 181–97.

8 K. Snow, 'Malaria and Mosquitoes in Britain: the Effect of Global Climate Change', *European Mosquito Bulletin*, 4 (1999), pp. 17–25; A. McMichael, R. Woodruff and S. Hales, 'Climate Change and Human Health: Present and Future Risks', *The Lancet*, CCCLXVII (2009), pp. 859–69.

9 P. Reiter, 'From Shakespeare to Defoe: Malaria in England in the Little Ice Age', *Emerging Infectious Diseases*, VI (2000), pp. 1–11.

10 M. J. Dobson, 'History of Malaria in England', *Journal of the Royal Society of Medicine*, LXXXII, suppl. no. 17 (1989), pp. 3–7.

11 M. Humphreys, 'Kicking a Dying Dog: DDT and the Demise of Malaria in the American South, 1942–1950', *Isis*, LXXXVII (1996), pp. 1–17.

12 C. Gramiccia and P. F. Beales, 'The Recent History of Malaria Control and Eradication', in *Malaria: Principles and Practice of Malariology*, ed. W. H. Wernsdorfer and I. McGregor (Edinburgh, 1988), pp. 1,366–7.

13 W. A. Hawley et al., '*Aedes albopictus* in North America: Probable Introduction in Used Tires from Northern Asia', *Science*, CCXXXVI

(1987), pp. 1,114–16.

14 P. Gérardin et al.,'Estimating Chikungunya Prevalence in La
Réunion Island Outbreak by Serosurveys: Two Methods for Two
Critical Times of the Epidemic', *BMC Infectious Diseases*, VIII
(2008), p. 99.

15 A. M. Dondorp et al., 'Fake Antimalarials in Southeast Asia
are a Major Impediment to Malaria Control: Multinational
Cross-sectional Survey on the Prevalence of Fake Antimalarials',
Tropical Medicine and International Health, IX (2004), pp. 1,241–6.

11 THE MOSQUITO LEGACY

1 WHO Global Malaria Programme, *World Malaria Report 2010*
(Geneva, 2010).

2 'Actress Stone raises fast million' (29 January 2005), at
www.bbc.co.uk/news, accessed 1 November 2011.

3 'Celebrities Join Save the Children on World Malaria Day'
(25 April 2008), at www.savethechildren.org.uk, accessed
1 November 2011.

4 J. Fang, 'A World Without Mosquitoes', *Nature*, CDLXVI (2010),
pp. 432–4.

Select Bibliography

Aardema, V., *Why Mosquitoes Buzz in People's Ears: A West African Tale* (New York, 1975)

Adcock, F. and J. Simms, eds, *The Oxford Book of Creatures* (Oxford, 1995)

Alcock, A., *Entomology for Medical Officers* (London, 1920)

Austen, E. E., *Blood-sucking Flies, Ticks, etc and How to Collect Them* (London, 1904)

—, *Illustrations of British Blood-sucking Flies* (London, 1906)

Banks, J., *Journal of the Right Hon. Sir Joseph Banks during Captain Cook's First Voyage in H.M.S. Endeavour in 1768–71 to Terra del Fuego, Otahite, New Zealand, Australia, The Dutch East Indies, etc.* (London, 1896)

Beavis, I. C., *Insects and Other Invertebrates in Classical Antiquity* (Exeter, 1988)

Bowman, M., *de Havilland Mosquito*, Crowood Aviation Series (Marlborough, 2005)

Boyce, R. W., *Mosquito or Man? The Conquest of the Tropical World* (London, 1910)

Burr, M., *The Insect Legion: The Significance of the Insignificant* (London, 1939)

Burton, R. F., *Personal Narrative of a Pilgrimage to Al-Madinah and Meccah*, memorial edn (London, 1893)

Carson, R., *Silent Spring* (Boston, MA, 1962)

Cheeseman, R. E., *In Unknown Arabia* (London, 1926)

Clark, J.M.F., *Bugs and the Victorians* (New Haven, CT, 2009)

Cohen, S. S., *Yankee Sailors in British Gaols: Prisoners of War at Forton and Mill, 1777–1783* (Cranbury, NJ, 1995)

Defoe, D., *Tour through the Eastern Counties of England, 1722* (London, 1888)

Ealand, Charles Aubrey, *Insects and Man: An Account of the More Important Harmful and Beneficial Insects . . .* (London, 1915)

Edwards, F. W., H. Oldroyd and J. Smart, *British Blood-sucking Flies* (London, 1939)

Farr, M., *Tintin: The Complete Companion* (London, 2001)

Gillett, J. D., *Mosquitoes*, The World Naturalist Series (London, 1971)

Harris, J. R., *An Angler's Entomology* (London, 1952)

Hogg, J., *The Microscope: Its History, Construction, and Application: Being a Familiar Introduction to the Use of the Instrument, and the Study of Microscopical Science* (London, 1854)

Howard, L. O., *A History of Applied Entomology (Somewhat Anecdotal)* (Washington, DC, 1930)

James, D., *Mosquito: An Omnilingual Nosferatu Pictomunication Novel* (Marietta, GA, 2005).

Lang, W. D., *A Map Showing the Known Distribution in England and Wales of the Anopheline Mosquitoes, with Explanatory Text and Notes* (London, 1918)

Lawrence, D. H., *Birds, Beasts and Flowers* (London, 1923)

—, *Pansies: A Selection* (n.p., 1929).

Livingstone, D., *Missionary Travels and Researches in South Africa; Including a Sketch of Sixteen Years' Residence in the Interior . . .* (London, 1857)

MacCulloch, J., *Malaria: an Essay on the Production and Propagation of This Poison, and on the Nature and Localities of the Places by Which It Is Produced: with an Enumeration of the Diseases Caused by It, and of the Means of Preventing or Diminishing Them, Both at Home and in the Naval and Military Service* (London, 1827)

Marren, P., and R. Mabey, *Bugs Britannica* (London, 2010)

Moore Hogarth, A., *British Mosquitoes and How to Eliminate Them* (London, 1928)

Munro, L., *This is Ann: She's Dying to Meet You* (Washington, DC, 1943)

Ray, J., *The Wisdom of God Manifested in the Works of Creation* (London, 1691)

Rocco, F., *The Miraculous Fever Tree: The Cure that Changed the World* (London, 2003)

Smith, R. F., T. E. Mittler, and C. N. Smith, eds, *History of Entomology* (Palo Alto, CA, 1973)

Snow, K. R., *Mosquitoes*, Naturalists' Handbooks 14 (Slough, 1990)

Snowden, F. M., *The Conquest of Malaria: Italy, 1900–1962* (New Haven, CT, 2006)

Teixeira, Pedro, *The Travels of Pedro Teixeira; with His 'Kings of Marmuz', and Extracts from His 'Kings of Persia'*, trans. W. F. Sinclair, with further notes and intro. by D. Fergusson (London, 1902)

Theobald, F. V., *A Monograph of the Culicidae or Mosquitoes. Mainly Compiled from the Collections Received at the British Museum from Various Parts of the World, in Connection with the Investigation into the Cause of Malaria Conducted by the Colonial Office and the Royal Society* (London, 1901–10)

Thwaite, A., *Glimpses of the Wonderful: The Life of Philip Henry Gosse, 1810–1888* (London, 2002)

von Humboldt, A., and A. Bonplan, *Personal Narrative of Travels to the Equinoctal Regions of America During the Years 1799–1804*; written in French by A. von Humboldt, trans. and ed. T. Ross (London, 1852)

Wallace, A. R., *A Narrative of Travels on the Amazon and Rio Negro, with an Account of the Native Tribes and Observations on the Climate, Geology, and Natural History of the Amazon Valley* (London, 1853)

—, *The Malay Archipelago: The Land of the Urang-Utan and the Bird of Paradise. A Narrative of Travel with Studies of Man and Nature* (London, 1869)

Wallace, R., ed., *Eleanor Ormerod, LLD, Economic Entomologist: Autobiography and Correspondence* (London, 1904)

Waterton, C., *Wanderings in South America, The North-West of the United States, and the Antilles, in the Years 1812, 1816, 1820 & 1824* (London, 1891)

Webb, J.L.A., Jr, *Humanity's Burden: A Global History of Malaria* (New York, 2009)

Wernsdorfer, W. H., and I. McGregor, eds, *Malaria: Principles and Practice of Malariology* (Edinburgh, 1988)

Westwood, J. O., *The Entomologist's Text-Book: An Introduction to the Natural History, Structure, Physiology and Classification of Insects* (London, 1838)

Associations and Websites

MALARIA SITE
www.malariasite.com
History and aetiology of malaria

NOBEL PRIZE
www.nobelprize.org
The Nobel Prize site is littered with references to mosquitoes, malaria,
yellow fever and DDT

EUROPEAN MOSQUITO BULLETIN
http://e-m-b.org
The journal of the European Mosquito Control Association

PUBLIC-HEALTH PEST CONTROL
http://entomology.ifas.ufl.edu/fasulo/vector/chapter_03.htm
Chapter Three from the Public-Health Pesticide Applicator Training
Manual, produced by the University of Florida

AMERICAN MOSQUITO CONTROL ASSOCIATION
www.mosquito.org

BRITISH MOSQUITOES
www.britishmosquitoes.org.uk
UK mosquito recording scheme, port watch and nationwide
surveillance

WORLD HEALTH ORGANIZATION
www.who.int/malaria/en
WHO on malaria

GATES FOUNDATION
www.gatesfoundation.org/topics/Pages/malaria.aspx
Bill and Melinda Gates Foundation portal

MALARIA MUSEUM
www.malariamuseum.com
Off-beat items on mosquitoes and malaria

MALARIA STAMPS
www.malariastamps.com
Mosquitoes on postage stamps

Acknowledgements

Help, advice and good-natured criticism for this book has come from a bizarre ragtag of people I am pleased to count among my family, friends and Facebook acquaintances. My father Alfred Jones, as ever, gave me the usual encouragement, started me on the trail of endless themes and ideas, lent me several of his old books and found all the Biggles references. Penny Metal mined a rich vein of art sources linked to mosquitoes. Other ideas and sources have come from: Jamie Barclay, Max Barclay, Sofie Braüner, Paul Carney, Richard Daniels, David Hibling, Ron Johnson, Terry Lee, Bob Machin, Ian Marchant, Toby Murcott, Julie Sorenson, Philip Stott, Roz Taylor, Anna Valdiserri, Claudia Watts, Ian Whiteley and Paul Williams. Horniman Museum librarians April Yasamee and Helen Williamson were very helpful when I first started trawling through old books on travel and natural history. Finally, Jonathan Burt, the series editor, made some serious editing suggestions to an early draft, without which the book would never have been finished. Thank you one and all.

Photo Acknowledgements

The author and publishers wish to express their thanks to the below sources of illustrative material and/or permission to reproduce it. (Some locations uncredited in the captions for reasons of brevity are also given below.)

Photo Adenis/Sipa Press/Rex Features: p. 138; from Ulisse Aldrovandi, *De animalibus insectis Libri septum cum singulorum iconibus . . .* (Bologna, 1636): p. 16 (left); collection of the author: p. 134; photo author: p. 27; photo Jamie Barclay: p. 166; from Caspar Bauhinus, *De Hermaphroditorum monstrosorumque partuum natura . . .* (Oppenheim, 1614): p. 88; from Rupert W. Boyce, *Mosquito or Man? The Conquest of the Tropical World* (London, 1909): pp. 106, 107 (top); British Museum, London (photos © Trustees of the British Museum): pp. 19, 51; from Richard Brookes, *The Natural History of Insects, with their Properties and Uses in Medicine*, vol. IV (London, 1763): p. 17; photos CDC/Phanie/Rex Features: pp. 9, 39; from John Curtis, *British Entomology, being Illustrations and Descriptions of the Genera of Insects found in Great Britain and Ireland; containing Coloured Figures from Nature of the Most Rare and Beautiful Species, and in Many Instances of the Plants upon which they are Found*, vol. VIII (London, 1839): p. 16 (right); Detroit Institute of Arts: p. 137; photo © Dreamworks/Everett/Rex Features: p. 46; from C. A. Ealand, *Insects and Man: An Account of the more Important Harmful and Beneficial Insects, their Habits and Life-histories, being an Introduction to Economic Entomology for Students and General Readers* (London, 1915): pp. 107

(foot), 111, 112, 132, 133; from F. W. Edwards, H. Oldroyd and J. Smart, *British Blood-sucking Flies* (London, 1939): p. 114; supplied by Giant microbes.com: p. 27; from Emílio Augusto Goeldi, *Os Mosquitos no Pará : Reunião de quatro trabalhos sobre os mosquitos indígenas, principalmente as espécies que molestam o homem* (Pará, 1906): pp. 116–17, 124–5; from *Half Hours in the Tiny World* (London, 1880): p. 61; from *Harper's Weekly*: pp. 77 (XXVI/431: 8 July 1882), 80 (XXV/800: 26 November 1881); photo © Henrik_L/2012 iStock International Inc.: p. 6; from John Hill, *The Book of Nature; or, The History of Insects: Reduced to distinct Classes, confirmed by particular Instances, Displayed in the Anatomical Analysis of many Species . . .* (London, 1758): p. 23 (left); from A. Moore Hogarth, *British Mosquitoes and How to Eliminate Them* (London, 1928): p. 122; from Jabez Hogg, *The Microscope: Its History, Construction, and Application: Being a Familiar Introduction to the Use of the Instrument, and the Study of Microscopical Science* (London, 1854): p. 32; from Dan James, *Mosquito* (Cleveland, Ohio, 2005), by permission of Dan James: p. 36; photo Alex Khroustalev: p. 26; photos Library of Congress, Washington, DC: pp. 50, 62, 64, 65, 80, 165; from L. C. Miall, *The Natural History of Aquatic Insects . . .* (London, 1895): p. 34; photo Stan Milosevic: p. 66; photos MosquitoZone Corporation: pp. 148, 149; Musée d'Orsay, Paris: pp. 82, 135; photo Jennifer Podis/Rex Features: p. 59; courtesy G. Poinar, Jr: p. 21; from *Puck*: pp. 62 (LXVI/1693: 11 August 1909), 165 (LXXII/1847: 24 July 1912); from Fritz Schaudinn, *Studien über krankheitserregende Protozoen. II. Plasmodium vivax (Grassi & Feletti), der Erreger des Tertianfiebers beim Menschen . . .* (Berlin, 1903): p. 97; from G. Z. Shaw, *General Zoology*, vol. VI (London, 1806): p. 23 (right); from John Smart, *A Handbook for the Identification of Insects of Medical Importance* (London, 1943): p. 115; photo courtesy of the US Center for Disease Control and Prevention: p. 182; courtesy the US National Library of Medicine, Bethesda, Maryland (History of Medicine Division): pp. 77, 89, 110, 144, 146, 150, 153; from Alfred Russel Wallace, *Darwinism: An Exposition of the Theory of Natural Selection, with Some of Its Applications* (London, 1889): p. 71 (left); from Alfred Russel Wallace, *A Narrative of Travels on the Amazon and Rio Negro, with an Account of the Native Tribes, and Observations on the Climate, Geology, and Natural History of the Amazon Valley* (London, 1889): p. 71 (right); photo James L. A. Webb, Jr: p. 140; Wellcome Library, London: pp. 48 (Ephemera Collection), 74, 88, 136, 147; Werner Forman Archive: p. 18; from *Wild Oats* (xv/190: August 1876): p. 50; photos Zoological Society of London: pp. 16, 23 (left), 116–17, 124–5, 127, 130.

Index